THE DEATH
OF A NATION

By
John A. Stormer

LIBERTY BELL PRESS
P. O. Box 32   Florissant, Missouri

THE DEATH OF A NATION

A LIBERTY BELL BOOK

First Printing, April, 1968
Second Printing, May, 1968
Third Printing, May, 1968

Liberty Bell Books are published by
THE LIBERTY BELL PRESS

P. O. Box 32

Florissant, Missouri

Printed in The United States of America

ABOUT THE AUTHOR

John Stormer's first book, *None Dare Call It Treason,* ranks fifth among all-time paperback best sellers. It is, according to *The New York Times,* the biggest selling political paperback book in history. Published in 1964, it has sold over 7-million copies.

The book was viciously attacked by liberal politicians, professors, and preachers. Most of the attacks stemmed from the "research" of one group which claimed the book was "discredited" because of inaccuracies (principally typographical errors in dates and page numbers) in 11 of 819 footnotes. The charges were successfully refuted by the author in his publication, *Anatomy of a Smear,* and by such major newspapers as the *Indianapolis Star,* the *Richmond News Leader* and others. None of the facts in the book has been proved wrong.

Stormer has served on the Missouri Republican State Committee and was state chairman of the Missouri Federation of Young Republicans (1962-64). He was a member of the Missouri delegation to the Republican Convention which nominated Barry Goldwater in 1964.

He has been licensed to preach the Gospel by Lackland Road Baptist Church in Overland, Missouri where he is a member and deacon. He is a member of the executive committee of the International Council of Christian Churches, a world-wide organization of 122 Bible-believing denominations which are not affiliated with the liberal National and World Councils of Churches.

A native of Altoona, Pa., he attended the Pennsylvania State University and graduated from California's San Jose State College in 1954 after Korean War Service as an Air Force historian. A member of Sigma Delta Chi, the professional journalism society, he lives in a suburb of St. Louis, Mo., with his wife and 9-year old daughter.

Since 1965 he has visited Vietnam twice and has toured Korea and other world trouble spots on fact-finding missions.

CONTENTS

We Are At War With Communism ⸺ 9

The War In The Streets ⸺ 24

The War In Vietnam ⸺ 43

Why Are Our Leaders Betraying Us? ⸺ 56

Communism, Youth and The New Morality ⸺ 67

The War In The Churches ⸺ 90

Nothing New Under The Sun ⸺ 123

If Communism Takes Over ⸺ 132

Can America Be Saved? ⸺ 140

Are We Nearing The End of the Age? ⸺ 152

DEDICATION AND FOREWORD

My first book, *None Dare Call It Treason,* was dedicated to my daughter, Holly, with the hope that her future "might be as bright as mine was at age five." Holly is now nine years old and the world situation is ever so much worse.

Daniel Webster foresaw the death walk which America is taking. He warned about it in a Fourth of July speech in Concord, Massachusetts in 1806. Webster said:

> When we speak of preserving the constitution, we mean not the paper on which it is written, but the spirit which dwells in it. Government may lose all of the real character, its genius, its temper without losing its appearance.

> Republicanism, unless you guard it, will creep out of its case of parchment, like a snake out of its skin. You may have despotism under the name of a Republic.

> You may look on a government, and see it possesses all the external modes of freedom, and yet finding nothing of the essence, the vitality, of freedom in it; just as you may contemplate an embalmed body, where art hath preserved proportion and form, amid nerves without action, and veins void of blood.

American needs a rebirth of the political and spiritual principles which were the "nerves" and "blood" of the Republic for almost 200 years. This book looks at what they were . . . and what we have become.

JOHN A. STORMER
Florissant, Missouri

The wicked shall be turned into hell,
and all nations that forget God.

— PSALM 9:17

Chapter I

We are at War with Communism

> *Lo, I will bring a nation upon you from afar,*
> *O house of Israel, saith the Lord: it is a mighty*
> *nation, it is an ancient nation, a nation whose*
> *language thou knowest not, neither under-*
> *standest what they say.*
>
> — *Jeremiah 5:15*

TWO WEEKS after Lee Harvey Oswald killed President Kennedy on the streets of Dallas, Texas, FBI Chief J. Edgar Hoover warned America with these words:

> We are at war with communism and the sooner every red-blooded American realizes this the safer we will be.[1]

The communists are waging their war against the United States on many fronts — with a variety of weapons. Fire-bombs and sniper bullets are used in the streets of America — missiles and MIGs in Vietnam. Filthy books, dirty movies, and burned draft cards are weapons in the communist war to corrupt America's youth. Less spectacular, but equally deadly battles are being fought with legal briefs before the Supreme Court of the United States.

J. Edgar Hoover issued his warning in December 1963. Since then . . .

> . . . Red bullets have killed three times more Americans in Vietnam than were killed in the Revolutionary War, the War of 1812, the Mexican War, and the Spanish-American War combined.[2]

As these Americans died in Vietnam, firebomb throwing mobs, led by communist-agitated and trained revolutionaries, killed over 150 people, injured several thousand others and destroyed property worth $1-billion in 100 American cities.

America is not winning the war with communism because America's people seem strangely unable — or unwilling — to face the fact that we are at war. America is losing the war with communism because the President, the Congress, and the Supreme Court won't decide which side they should be on. Unbelievable? Consider this strange sequence of events:

On July 28, 1965, President Lyndon Johnson told a nation-wide TV audience that America was undertaking a massive military buildup in Vietnam to deal the communists "death and desolation" if that must be the path to a just peace.[3] Within 30 months, nearly 150,000 young Americans were killed or wounded in the effort.

By sending these men to fight in Southeast Asia, President Johnson seemingly recognized communism as an enemy. However, as they suffered and died his administration . . .

> . . . made agreements to sell or give the Soviet Union and her communist satellites hundreds of millions of dollars worth of food, electronic computers, chemical plants, oil refinery equipment, airborne radar apparatus, jet aircraft engines, machine tools for an $800-million auto assembly plant, and military rifles.[4]

Each of these shipments were designated as "non-strategic" by Washington. However, they all increased the war-making potential of Soviet industry at a time when Russian factories were the major source of supply for the guns, bullets, MIG airplanes and surface-to-air missiles the Viet Cong was using to kill thousands of Americans.

As young Americans fought *against* communism in Vietnam, the Supreme Court of the United States . . .

> . . . gave communists the right to teach in America's public schools by declaring a New York state law against communist teachers unconstitutional. Jobs in defense plants were also opened to members of communist action groups by Supreme Court decision.[5]

As young Americans died fighting against communism in Vietnam, President Johnson, the State Department, and the U.S. Senate . . .

> . . . granted the Soviet Union the right to open diplomatic offices in a dozen additional American cities. The treaty was approved even though J. Edgar Hoover had warned earlier that existing Red embassies are the principal bases for the communist espionage network in America.[6]

At a time when the Soviet Union was supplying the MIGs and missiles which were killing American boys in

Vietnam, the U.S. Senate approved a treaty with communist Russia which...

> ...denies America the right to fully develop, test, and deploy advanced space-type weapons needed to strengthen our defenses in the future. No inspection provisions were included to safeguard against possible destruction of America by a sneak attack if the communists cheat.[7]

Efforts to stop foreign aid *to the communists* and their allies have been regularly defeated in Congress. On November 8, 1967, Congressman H. R. Gross (R-Iowa) tried to amend the foreign aid bill to prohibit American foreign aid grants to nations which trade with North Vietnam. Congress defeated the amendment by a vote of 200 to 196.[8]

The time has come for Americans to ask, "Which side are they on?"

THE WAR IN THE STREETS

Washington follows the same pattern of "fight them with one hand and aid them with the other" in dealing with the agitators who are fomenting the war in America's streets. Billions of dollars have been appropriated by Congress to finance a "war on poverty." Such spending is supposed to eliminate the slum conditions which agitators exploit to start riots.

Any merit such an approach might have had was cancelled out when communists and other agitators were hired to administer the "war on poverty." Dozens of agitators paid with federal funds were directly involved in provoking the disastrous wave of riots which spread across America in the summer of 1967.[9] Washington, though warned in advance of the activities of the agitators, refused to take action. On May 25, 1967, six weeks before the rioting broke out in Newark, N.J., Police Director Dominick A. Spina sent Sargent Shriver, director of the U.S. Office of Economic Opportunity, this telegram:

> I strongly protest the use of resources and manpower from the United Community Corporation, an agency of the Office of Economic Opportunity, for the purpose of fomenting and agitating against the organized and democratic government of Newark.
>
> The United Community Corporation has rented . . . vehicles to use to agitate against the Planning Board of the

City of Newark and the Board of Education. Persons employed by UCC have told us they have been threatened with loss of their jobs if they do not participate in picketing and demonstrations against the agencies and government of Newark. I feel that this is directly opposed to the purpose of the anti-poverty funds and ask that such practices be stopped immediately. The acceleration of this kind of practice by this anti-poverty agency will undoubtedly lead to riots and anarchy in our city. I request immediate response.[10]

Shriver rejected the pleas of the Newark police official. Six weeks later riots and anarchy did come to Newark. Property worth millions of dollars was burned and looted. After 26 persons were killed and 1000 injured, the flames lighted in Newark spread to Detroit, Milwaukee, Minneapolis and 40 other American cities.

In the aftermath of the riots, it was disclosed that in city after city across America war-on-poverty officials and employees helped fan the flames of rioting, looting and violence. In Newark, police charged that literature telling how to make Molotov cocktails (firebombs) was produced on mimeograph machines in Newark war-on-poverty offices. Commenting on the report, the syndicated columnists Novak and Evans said:

> Even the liberals concede this may be so and should be investigated.[11]

Whether facing the war in Vietnam or the war in the streets, Washington fights communism with one hand — and finances it with the other.

THE REAL THREAT

The real threat to America's future comes not from doublemindedness in the White House, communist-agitated mobs, nor a Supreme Court which opens public schools to communist teachers while declaring Bible reading and prayer unconstitutional. Apathetic citizens who read of near-treasonable acts on the front pages of daily newspapers and do nothing are the real problem. If during World War II, for example, a member of the U.S. Senate had encouraged college students to collect blood for Hitler's SS Troops, it is doubtful whether the American people would have bothered with the formality of a treason trial.

In 1965, while the communists were killing and wounding 1000 Americans a week in Vietnam, Senator Robert Kennedy

(D-NY) told students at the University of California that donating their blood for the communist North Vietnamese would be in "the oldest tradition of this country."[12] His statement — in the tradition of Benedict Arnold — provoked little more protest than a few mild editorials in conservative newspapers.

During an 8000-mile cross-country tour in the summer of 1967 *New York Times* columnist James Reston sensed the deep-seated apathy with which Americans are afflicted. He wrote:

> If you go across the country and talk at random to anybody you meet about the riots and war, you get a very confused and even contradictory impression . . . In general, people are prosperous and remote from the crises at home and abroad. They are vaguely troubled about Detroit and Saigon, but the fighting does not directly affect the lives of the majority and anyway, they don't seem to feel they can do anything about it.[13]

People are prosperous. They don't like to face unpleasantness. As long as the average American has money in his pocket, he ignores any sign that warns of serious trouble in Washington — unless his son gets sent to Vietnam, his wife gets mugged or raped on a dark street, or a mob burns his home down. Such an attitude can destroy a country built on the concept of "government of the people, by the people, and for the people."

ALL ACCORDING TO PLAN

Why can't the United States — the world's top military power — win a war against a backward little country the size of the state of Missouri? Why can't authorities maintain order in America's major cities? Why won't the American people face their problems? *What's wrong in America?* United Press International asked that question in a special survey of national problems in November 1967. The article started:

> Rioters burn and loot. Demonstrators defile the flag and curse the President. Young men answer the call to arms with, "Hell no, we won't go!" Mongers of hate spread their poison. Teen-agers turn to drugs and sex. What's wrong in America? Is the nation going to hell, led pell mell by a generation of mixed up, turned on, dropped out youth?[14]

Looking for answers, the United Press asked many prominent Americans, "What's wrong?" From their responses, these danger areas were pinpointed:

> There is a lack of national will . . . there is hostilty between negroes and whites . . . between cities and suburbs . . . between rich and poor . . . So-called peacemakers have been caught up in virulent, irrational hatred . . .
> The country is flooded . . . sometimes with the sanctions of the courts — with sexy books, dirty movies, and profanity on the stage . . . The theologians quarrel among themselves as to the nature of God and whether He is alive or dead . . . the theme of the day is to take all you can regardless of how you get it — and a lot of this attitude is seeping down from high places.

The United Press writer, Harry Ferguson, described these and other signs which scream *DANGER!* Then he shrugged his shoulders and hopefully concluded that, even so, America is basically sound, although. . .

> . . . it suffers from some illogical, disruptive ferment.

Four years earlier, FBI Director J. Edgar Hoover warned America about the "yeast" which is causing the "disruptive ferment," when he said:

> We are at war with communism and the sooner every red-blooded American realizes it the safer we will be.

The communists are waging their war to win the world by following detailed plans carefully spelled out over 50 years ago by Lenin, the man who brought communism to Russia. In summary, Lenin's plan states:

> First, we will take eastern Europe, then the masses of Asia, then we will encircle the United States which will be the last bastian of capitalism. We will not have to attack. It will fall into our hands like an overripe fruit.

The stalemated wars in Korea and Vietnam, rising hostility between negroes and whites, Washington's policy of fighting communism with one hand and aiding it with the other, the riots, and the "don't care" attitude of most Americans are warnings that the "fruit is ripening" *according to plan.*

The communists were given the nations of eastern Europe at the conference table at Yalta in 1945.[15] With the help of the U.S. State Department, they conquered China in 1950 to dominate the Asian land mass.[16] Today, the communists are implementing a three-pronged attack to accomplish the final goal of Lenin's plan — the enslavement of the United States. They are working to. . .

> . . . create such violent and widespread racial strife and turmoil in U.S. cities that America's *ability* to resist will be destroyed.[17]

While working to paralyze America internally through domestic strife, the communists also plan to. . .

> . . . keep the United States involved in a continuing series of Korea and Vietnam-type brushfire wars. They hope the high cost in lives and money of a series of such no-win wars will eventually destroy America's *will* to resist.[18]

The Johnson Administration's answer for this dual Red offensive is the war of "containment" in Vietnam and a "war on poverty" at home — while aiding the communists in the Soviet Union. It has succeeded only in increasing the federal budget by 86% in four years — from $100-billion in 1964 to $186-billion in 1968.

The resulting massive deficits have been financed through inflation — expanded credit and printing press money. Between 1961 and 1966, the money supply in the U.S. was increased 47% by "creeping inflation."[19] By 1968, the American housewife felt the pinch whenever she went to the grocery store. The American dollar, weakened by inflation, was on the brink of destruction. In an article entitled, "The Rising Risk of Runaway Inflation," the *Reader's Digest* told why. It said:

> . . . inflation in the "creeping" stage is like a ship which, because of a small hole in her hull, is sinking at the rate of a foot an hour. But at last comes a moment of crisis. Then confidence in a nation's money can vanish overnight and, like the ship . . . it plunges suddenly toward the bottom.[20]

The article described how unbalanced budgets brought inflation to Germany after World War I. Once her treasury was low in gold and the budget still unbalanced, German inflation moved to the runaway stage. Within four years, the German mark, which had been worth 25¢ in 1919, declined in value until *four trillion* were needed to equal one dollar in buying power. The *Reader's Digest* told what happened:

> The German middle classes had lost all their savings. The value of every pension was wiped out. All security was gone. Then the people were ready to listen to any demagogue

who would voice their bitterness: his name was Adolf Hitler.[21]

By December 1967, foreign banks, business interests and governments were concerned enough about the stability and future value of the U.S. dollar that they increased their demands for payment of American obligations in gold instead of dollars. *About one twelfth of the total American gold supply disappeared in one month!* It was the sharpest drop in history.[22] President Johnson first announced restrictions on travel and investment abroad by Americans. Then, as predicted four years before in *None Dare Call It Treason,* the President asked Congress to remove the requirement that 25¢ in gold be kept on hand for each paper dollar issued.[23] All silver backing for paper money and the silver content of dimes and quarters had already been removed.[24] Removing the gold reserve requirement for paper money would free $11-billion in gold to meet foreign obligations, postponing the financial crisis *temporarily.* It would also open the door to runaway printing press inflation of the type that destroyed Germany. *None Dare Call It Treason* told how:

> Without the restraint imposed on the issuance of paper money by the gold reserve requirement, future national deficits could be financed with printing press dollars. Printing press inflation, as contrasted with the gradual longterm debasement of currency, could reduce the value of the dollar to 10 cents or even one cent within months.

> Such runaway inflation would destroy confidence in free enterprise and representative government. The insurance and savings of millions of individuals, rich and poor, would be wiped out.

> The resulting "national emergency" could be used as justification for abolishing the constitutional processes and establishing a totalitarian, socialistic government. The Americans who might be expected to oppose such a takeover would have no resources to finance opposition. Their savings would have been confiscated by runaway inflation.[25]

As fantastic as it may seem — it would all be *according to plan.* Lenin said:

> The surest way to overthrow an existing social order is to debauch the currency.[26]

Communists have already used inflation as a weapon in their conquest of Hungary and China and in destroying

the government of Bolivia.[27] Must it happen in America?
The *Reader's Digest* said:

> To prevent this calamity we need a balanced budget, a
> sober credit policy, and an abandonment of the delusion
> that printing press money is the cause of real prosperity.
> If this is temporarily painful and takes courage, it should
> be far less painful than runaway inflation — in the longrun
> our only other choice.[28]

THEIR SECRET WEAPON

Do Americans have the "courage" to take the "temporarily
painful" steps necessary to avoid runaway inflation? Are there
enough Americans with the "moral stamina" to put the nation — and perhaps their own families — on a "pay as you
go" basis? The communists are certain that Americans don't
have what it takes. They are confident because they have
been undermining America's moral foundations for over 50
years. Following Lenin's blueprint, they have worked to. . .

> . . . make America's people so rotten and decadent morally
> that they will not resist an eventual communist takeover.[29]

The communists are getting a lot of help from non-com-
munists. That too is *according to plan*. J. Edgar Hoover has
pointed out. . .

> . . . it is basic to communist strategy to further com-
> munist objectives with non-communist hands.[30]

Communist successes can be measured in a number of
ways. The *Reader's Digest* reported in May 1964 that. . .

> . . . the smut industry is approaching an estimated two-
> billion-dollar-a-year volume, rapidly turning this country
> into the pornographic capital of the world.

A committee of the U.S. Senate investigating juvenile
delinquency reported that. . .

> . . . the moral fiber of the country is being undermined
> by a deluge of vile and filthy books, pictures and other
> pornographic material. Worst of all, up to 75 percent of it
> falls into the hands of minors.[31]

In high schools across America students are required to
read such trash as J. D. Salinger's *The Catcher In The Rye*,
which has four-letter words sprinkled on nearly every page.
On college campuses, students are being exposed to unbe-

lievable filth. A California newspaper reviewed "a lewd, smut-ridden play" produced by the Drama Department at California State College at Fullerton in November 1967. The review said:

> "The Beard," a play by Michael McClure produced by students at California State College at Fullerton . . . is 60 minutes of verbalizing riddled by four letter words which leads to the final jolt — performance of an oral sex act on stage in view of the audience.[32]

The shocked reviewer said, "Where is the message and what is the value of such a production?"

The California State Legislature assigned a special committee to investigate. Finding the reports to be true, it recommended that faculty members responsible for staging the play be fired. In its report, the investigating committee said that it was. . .

> . . . appalled by the fact that the President of the College clearly stated that he would take no action of any kind, either against any person or the distribution of any kind of material on the campus, unless and until it had been proven to be illegal and so declared by a court. . . . The Committee feels that . . . the administration is placing its view of academic freedom above morality and community responsibility.[33]

The college president, when questioned by the committee, said that because a person's morals are established before they get to college that colleges neither could *nor should* do anything to influence the moral climate surrounding students.[34]

Five members of the California Legislature from the Fullerton area resigned from the college's advisory board. In resigning they said:

> We cannot condone or tolerate the use of tax-supported educational facilities for public demonstrations of oral copulation whether simulated or real. We cannot continue to lend our names to an organization of "friends" of a college where this kind of moral degradation receives faculty approval.[35]

With young people being subjected to such influences. . .

> . . . half of all college girls have sexual relations before marriage . . . births to unmarried teenagers have increased 39% in five years . . . one out of three brides are pregnant at the altar . . . and venereal diseases among teenagers have increased 255% in six years.[36]

HOW ARE THEY DOING?

By 1968, communists could rejoice at their success in creating racial tension and turmoil in America's major cities. They could look with hopeful anticipation at the stalemated war in Vietnam and the financial crisis it was creating in Washington. They can survey the moral and spiritual decay in the United States with a confidence that they will not have to attack because America. . .

   . . . will fall into their hands like an overripe fruit.

IS THERE ANY HOPE?

Any sober, realistic survey of communist successes, can only lead the concerned citizen to a cry of, "Can anything be done? Can America be saved?" Those are questions that May Craig, longtime lady member of TV's *Meet The Press* panel, tried to answer in a column she penned for the Portland, Maine *Sunday Telegram* on February 9, 1964. Mrs. Craig wrote:

> Unless there is a change, deep-down in the American people, a genuine crusade against self indulgence and immorality, public and private, then we are witnesses to the decline and fall of the American Republic.

She looked at the sickness of America — in people and in the government — and warned:

> Death on the highways . . . cheating from top to bottom in our society, get rich quick, break-up of the family, faltering foreign policy, reckless debt — these have destroyed nations before us. Why should we think we can take that path and change history?

In a stinging indictment of America's "faltering foreign policy" Mrs. Craig detailed Washington's failures this way.

> Round the world they think they can take our money with one hand and slap us in the face with the other . . .
> Because it is unpleasant to think of unpleasant things, we say the Soviet Union is changing its determination to bury us. Red China is bad, of course, but maybe Russia is not.
> Half-heartedly we send American men to die in jungles, where we do not have the guts to go in to win or stay out. We sell wheat to Russia to save her from a demonstration that Communism cannot produce enough food for its own people . . .

We sign test-ban treaties with known enemies, known defaulters on treaties, that we will not test as we may need to. Why should we rest our defense on such an agreement?

May Craig offered a two-point program to prevent the "decline and fall of the American Republic." She wrote:

> First, everyone of us has to clean out weakness and selfishness and immorality of all types. Then, choose leaders who with strength and principle and intelligence will lead us to where we can have self respect and the respect of others.

In closing, she asked:

> Would we elect such a man if he campaigned on such a platform?

American voters answered May Craig's question in November 1964 with a landslide rejection of a man who campaigned for the presidency on such a platform. American conservatives, seeking political solutions for America's sickness, tried to elect a leader of principle and strength before the hearts of the people had been purged of "weakness, selfishness, and immorality." They did not succeed because America's problem is not basically political — it is a moral problem.

One of the founding fathers foresaw the possibility that moral decay might someday destroy America. Thomas Jefferson issued this warning almost 150 years ago.

> Yes, we did produce a near perfect Republic. But will they keep it, or will they, in the enjoyment of plenty, lose the memory of freedom? Material abundance without character is the surest way to destruction.

A French political philosopher who visited our shores when America was a new young nation left a similar warning. Alexis de Tocqueville said he came to the United States to learn what magic quality enabled a handful of people to defeat the mighty British Empire twice in 35 years. He looked for the greatness of America in her harbors and rivers, her fertile fields and boundless forests, mines and other natural resources. He studied America's schools, her Congress and her matchless Constitution without comprehending America's power. Not, he said, until he went into the churches of America and heard pulpits "aflame with righteousness" did he understand the secret of her genius and strength. De Tocqueville returned to France and wrote:

> America is great because America is good, and if America ever ceases to be good, America will cease to be great.[37]

America sends her sons to fight communism while aiding the communists who supply the bullets they dodge. America tolerates court-ordered bans on prayer and Bible reading in the schools while permitting communists to teach. America has ceased to be good. Will America soon cease to be great? Even if there were no communist threat, growing moral decay and spiritual bankruptcy will destroy America from within.

WHAT'S GONE WRONG?

In the enjoyment of plenty, Americans have forgotten that they have done very little to deserve all they have. We are enjoying the fruits of a heritage won for us by past generations — a heritage we did nothing to win. There are many similarities between America today and the nation of Israel which God took into the promised land 3500 years ago. As the children of Israel were about to receive their inheritance, God, through Moses, told them that they could expect...

> ... great and goodly cities which thou buildest not, and houses full of good things which thou fillest not, and wells digged, which thou diggest not, vineyards and olive trees which thou plantedest not ...
> ... a good land, a land of brooks of water ... a land of wheat and barley, and vines ... a land wherein thou shalt eat breat without scarceness, thou shalt not lack anything in it. ... (Deuteronomy 6:10-11, 8:7-9)

The Israelites were given a land flowing with "milk and honey" by God. Americans also have great material blessings — in a land of freedom, prosperity and opportunity. Americans lack for very little — not because of their own merit — but because God caused them to be born in America rather than in some other land. If you lived in almost any other country taking a drink of water could mean risking dysentery, typhoid or something worse.

There are dangers in the enjoyment of plenty. Men can quickly fall into an attitude of "eat, drink, and be merry" and forget to protect the freedom which makes prosperity possible. Thomas Jefferson warned of this danger 150 years ago — just as Moses warned his charges 3500 years before. After telling the Israelites of the blessings they'd find in the promised land, Moses warned:

> When thou hast eaten and art full, then thou shalt bless the Lord thy God for the good land which he hath given thee.
> Beware that thou forget not the Lord thy God, in not keeping his commandments, and his judgments, and his statutes, which I command thee this day:
> Lest when thou hast eaten and art full, and hast built goodly houses, and dwelt therein:
> And when thy herds and thy flocks multiply, and thy silver and thy gold is multiplied, and all that thou hast is multiplied;
> Then thine heart be lifted up, and thou forget the Lord thy God, which has brought thee forth out of the land of Egypt, from the house of bondage;
> And thou say in thine heart, My power and the might of mine hand hath gotten me this wealth. (Deuteronomy 8:10-14, 17)

That's our danger today. So many believe that prosperity is the result of our own efforts, our system of government, or a program of planned inflation. Moses' warning to his people holds true today, however:

> But thou shalt remember the Lord thy God: For it is He that giveth thee power to get wealth . . .
> And it shall be, if thou do at all forget the Lord thy God, and walk after other gods, and serve them, and worship them, I testify against you this day that ye shall surely perish. (Deuteronomy 8:18-19)

America is walking after the false gods of pleasure and materialism — sex and security. America has forgotten the true and living God who has given us the power to get wealth — and the freedom to enjoy it. Our coins still carry the slogan, "In God We Trust," but prayer and Bible reading is banned from our schools. The pledge of allegiance to the American flag still says we are "one nation under God" but crime statistics, growing rates of alcoholism, drug addiction, divorce and corruption in high places make the words an empty slogan rather than a reality.

How many Americans drop to their knees daily to thank "the Lord thy God for the good land which He hath given them" as Moses commanded? Do you?

As America's people have turned their backs on a day-to-day living relationship with the living God, they have also forgotten their political responsibilities as well.

Is there any hope for America? That great soldier, General Douglas MacArthur, blueprinted the two possible paths America can follow. MacArthur said:

> History fails to record a single precedent in which nations subject to moral decay have not passed into political and economic decline. There has been either a spiritual awakening to overcome the moral lapse, or a progressive deterioration leading to ultimate national disaster.

Can America be saved? The Bible, the testimony of history, and the sober, considered words of General MacArthur, all warn that unless America turns back to God, she is doomed.

Nations, however, don't turn to God — or away from Him. Only individuals can.

Chapter II

The War in the Streets— Destroying America's Ability to Resist

. . . the whole land shall be desolate . . . thy cities shall be laid waste . . . and when thou art spoiled, what wilt thou do?
— *Jeremiah 4:7, 27, 30*

THE RIOTS, LOOTING, sniper attacks on police and massive civil disturbances which have racked American cities since 1964 are part of the Communist program for destroying America's ability to resist.

In February 1967, FBI Chief J. Edgar Hoover told a committee of the U.S. Congress:

> Communists and other subversives and extremists strive and labor ceaselessly to precipitate racial trouble and take advantage of racial discord in this country. Such elements were active in exploiting and aggravating the riots, for example, in Harlem, Watts, Cleveland and Chicago.[1]

Other law enforcement agencies and judicial commissions have issued similar warnings. On the fourth day of the Harlem riots in 1964, acting New York city mayor Paul Screvane stated that "known communists" had been involved in the inflammatory rallies and meetings which preceded the riots and that Communist money had probably financed some of the demonstrations.[2] Former communist Philip Abbot Luce confirmed Screvane's charges. In his book, *Road To Revolution*, written after he left the conspiracy, Luce told how he and other communists were "in the center of these riots and did everything possible to expand and extend the riot conditions." He said:

> All of us, as good Communists, were responsible for some work in the riots and each of us longed for the possibility

that Harlem would herald the beginning of a nationwide guerilla war.[4]

The Cuyahoga County Special Grand Jury which investigated the 1966 summer riots in Cleveland reported:

> This jury finds that the outbreak of lawlessness and disorder was both organized, precipitated, and exploited by a relatively small group of trained and disciplined professionals at this business. They were aided and abetted, willingly or otherwise, by misguided people of all ages and colors, many of whom are avowed believers in violence and extremism, and some of whom are also either members or officers of the Communist Party.[5]

That the communists work to exploit and aggravate racial tensions and rioting and terrorism in America's cities is no surprise to any student of communist theory and tactics. In 1902, Lenin wrote this guide for future communists:

> We must go among all classes of people as theoreticians, as propagandists, as agitators, and as organizers. . . . The principal thing, of course, is propaganda and agitation among all strata of people.[6]

As early as 1925, the Communist Party, U.S.A. instructed its members:

> The aim of our party in our work among the Negro masses is to create a powerful proletarian movement which will fight and lead the struggle of the Negro race against exploitation and oppression in every form and which will be a militant part of the revolutionary movement of the whole American working class . . . and connect them with the struggles of national minorities and colonial peoples of all the world and thereby further the cause of the world revolution and the dictatorship of the proletariat.[7]

J. Edgar Hoover has outlined the goals for communists working among Negroes. He said:

> Communists seek to advance the cause of communism by injecting themselves into racial situations and in exploiting them (1) to intensify the frictions between Negroes and whites to "prove" that discrimination against minorities is an inherent defect of the capitalist system, (2) to foster domestic disunity by dividing Negroes and whites into antagonistic, warring factions, (3) to undermine and destroy established authority, (4) to incite Negro hostility toward law and order, (5) to encourage and foment racial strife and riotous activity, and (6) to portray the Communist movement as

the "champion" of social protest and the only force capable
of ameliorating the conditions of the Negro and the
oppressed.[8]

How do the communists achieve these goals among Negroes? J. Edgar Hoover answered this question in an earlier
appearance before the House Appropriations Subcommittee.
Mr. Hoover said that the Communist Party . . .

> . . . strives only to exploit what are often legitimate
> Negro complaints and grievances for the advancement of
> communist objectives. Controversial or potentially controver-
> sial racial issues are deliberately and avidly seized upon
> by the Communists for the fullest possible exploitation.
> Racial incidents are magnified and dramatized by the
> Communists in an effort to generate racial tensions. As a
> result, such campaigns are actually utilized as a stepping
> stone to extend Communist influence among the Negroes.[9]

Mr. Hoover summarized the results of Communist efforts
to exploit the Negro with these words:

> The cumulative effect of almost 50 years of Communist
> Party activity in the United States cannot be minimized,
> for it has contributed to disrupting race relations in this
> country and has exerted an insidious influence on the life
> and times of our Nation. . . . The net result of agitation
> and propaganda by Communist and other subversive and
> extremist elements has been to create a climate of conflict
> between the races in this country and to poison the at-
> mosphere.[10]

HOW DO RIOTS START?

Riots stemming from conflict between the races killed
nearly 150 persons and injured thousands of others between
1964 and 1967. Over $1-billion worth of property was de-
stroyed. As Americans started to ask, "Why?" evidence
mounted that the upheaval was not purely the result of
"spontaneous combustion." Undoubtedly minority group unemployment, poor housing, and racial discrimination exists
in America. However, city slums have always been plagued
by sub-standard conditions without riots and bloodshed resulting. Actually, conditions have improved measureably for
the Negro — and all Americans — in the last 15 years.

Gary, Indiana is probably typical of northern industrial
cities which have been plagued by racial strife. A survey
of economic conditions in Gary during the summer of 1967

showed an annual income of $9215 for the average white family while Negro families average $7379.[11] As these figures show, differences do exist — but families with annual incomes of $7379 are not poverty stricken.

How and why, then, did the riots start?

Police officials from Cincinnati, Ohio, Nashville, Tennessee and other cities told the Senate Judicial Committee that racial harmony existed in their cities *until* outside agitators moved in. Cincinnati Police Chief Jacob W. Schott charged that four months of firebombing and guerilla-type violence followed an April 29 speech in which agitator Stokely Carmichael urged Negroes to "fight the police and burn the city."[12]

Nashville Police Captain John Sorace testified that an April 8, 1967 riot in his city followed a week of agitation by Stokely Carmichael, H. Rap Brown and other leaders of the Student Non-Violent Coordinating Committee (SNCC).[13]

An outbreak of violence in Dayton, Ohio followed a speech by H. Rap Brown who succeeded Carmichael as head of SNCC.[14] Brown spoke in East St. Louis, Illinois, on September 10, 1967. Four days later, the *St. Louis Post Dispatch* summed up what happened saying:

> In the four days since Brown's appearance at Lincoln Senior High School there have been almost 80 fires, most of them minor, 13 injuries, one death, and 49 arrests. Arson is suspected in many of the fires. No damage estimates have been made.[15]

Brown was also blamed for a riot in Cambridge, Maryland on July 24. Cambridge Police Chief Brice Kinnamon told Congress that a "highly imflammatory speech" by Brown was "the sole reason for our riot." Kinnamon said:

> The street was full of guns seconds after the speech. It was a well organized and well planned affair.[16]

The speech received national press coverage at the time. Brown told the Cambridge, Maryland crowd:

> . . . get a gun. I don't care if it's a BB gun with poisoned BB's. America has got to come around or black people are going to burn it down.[17]

As these police officials testified of the role agitators such as Carmichael and Brown played in sparking riots, Carmichael himself visited Castro's Cuba and said America's Negroes would wage a guerilla "fight to the death." In

Havana for a meeting of Latin American communist revolutionary leaders, Carmichael said:

> In Newark we applied the war tactics of the guerillas. We are preparing groups of urban guerillas for our defense in the cities. The price of these rebellions is a high price one must pay. This fight is not going to be a simple street meeting. It is going to be a fight to the death.[18]

In 1925, the Communist Party set out to make American Negroes "a militant part of the revolutionary movement" in America and then "connect them with the struggles of naional minorities and colonial peoples of all the world and thereby further the cause of world revolution." They are succeeding. After Carmichael's speech in Cuba, the national headquarters of the Student Non-Violent Coordinating Committee in New York announced that "our representative, Mr. Stokely Carmichael," was going to Hanoi, North Vietnam, to . . .

> . . . see for himself the savage aggression being carried out against that country by the United States.[19]

The testimony of the police chiefs and the boasts of Stokely Carmichael are collaborated by a detailed study of the 1967 Detroit riot done by a militant Negro civil rights activist. Louis Lomax, one of America's leading Negro authors, had his eyes opened by the activities of trained revolutionaries in Detroit. Lomax reported that the Detroit riot occured because . . .

> . . . an organized group, largely from outside the Detroit area, had been operating in the city more than a month. . . . this group had an assignment: burn and destroy.[20]

Lomax said the group was highly organized and well trained — "not thieves and arsonists in the ordinary sense of the words." They are instead, he said . . .

> . . . revolutionaries committed to the conclusion that the power structure does not have the moral fiber to repent for its socio-economic sins; that the only truly corrective measure is to leave the nation in ashes.
> The principal U.S. cities have been chosen as the initial battle ground simply because they afford the kind of cooperation by the innocent and uninformed that every such revolution needs.[21]

In his series of five articles,[22] Lomax told how these revolutionary agitators, posing as magazine salesmen, worked

through the Negro neighborhoods of Detroit, spreading hate
and poison. They laid a foundation of hate — and then
waited until an incident occured between a Negro and the
police which was used to spark the riot. Lomax told what
happened once the trouble started. He said:

> Methodically breaking store windows, the revolutionaries
> urged the milling Negro people to loot and steal. But — and
> at least a dozen observers confirmed this — the professionals
> did no looting of their own. They are not thieves. They are
> men at war, revolutionaries bent on reducing the nation to
> ashes.
>
> The looters unknowingly cooperated by having a happy
> time. The streets teemed with whites and colored who stole
> with abandon and glee. People came in cars from miles
> away and hauled off freezers, sofas, television sets and
> clothing.[23]

Why didn't the police stop the looting? When Dr. James
Boyce, a Negro professor at Wayne University, asked a
policeman that question, he was told:

> We're following orders . . .[24]

Lomax concluded that much of the rioting, burning and
looting was carried out by unknowing citizens who "joined
the fun" once the riots started. On the other hand, he said . . .

> . . . the hard core of sniper activity was highly organized.
> The link between the dedicated revolutionaries and the
> organized sniper is more philosophical than organizational.
> The snipers, on the whole, were Detroit's own sons — Black
> Power advocates who are trained in guerilla warfare.[25]

How do riots start? The testimony of J. Edgar Hoover,
police officials, and concerned Negroes clearly indicate that
subversive agitators provided the sparks which have started
the flames burning in America's cities. Congressman E. E.
Willis (D-La) said a report by staff investigators of the
House Committee on Un-American Activities . . .

> . . . clearly indicates that certain subversive elements
> have been involved in some of these riots and in creation
> of racial unrest generally.[26]

WIDESPREAD BLINDNESS

Despite the evidence and warnings, most prominent Americans refused to face the danger of communist exploitation
of the riots squarely. Roy Wilkins, longtime head of the

National Association for Advancement of Colored People
and a member of the commission President Johnson named
to investigate the riots, refused to brand Stokely Carmichael
as "dangerous." Ten days before Carmichael arrived in Cuba
to make his "fight to the death" speech, Wilkins told "Meet
The Press" TV cameras, "I don't consider Stokely a wild
one. I consider him a leader of the militants."

Illinois Governor Otto Kerner, chairman of the commission
President Johnson established to determine the cause of the
riots, showed a similar blindness or bias. As the investigation
got underway he announced that he did not believe that
an organized movement was behind the riots.[27]

With such preconceived ideas, Kerner would have been
barred from sitting on any jury in America. Even so, the
President appointed him to head the "fact-finding" commission which was to find the cause of the riots. It is not
surprising that after seven months of "fact-finding" Kerner's
commission reported that it could find no evidence of a
"conspiracy" or "plan" behind the riots. Kerner even mis-
used J. Edgar Hoover's name and reputation to back his
opinion that communists were not behind the riots. After
Hoover reported to a closed-door meeting of the commission,
Kerner told newsmen that the FBI Director had . . .

> . . . no intelligence on which to base any evidence of
> a conspiracy.[28]

Five days later, the *St. Louis Globe Democrat* reported
from Washington that . . .

> . . . FBI sources say that J. Edgar Hoover's views on the
> riots were not set forth fully when Illinois Gov. Otto Kerner
> gave newsmen a summary of his testimony following a
> closed door session with the President's riot investigating
> commission.
> They go so far as to say that the White House is using
> him to downplay the seriousness of alleged communist
> involvement. His sentiments, they (FBI sources) point out,
> are still along the line of his February testimony before the
> House Appropriations Committee. He said then that com-
> munists and other subversives and extremists were active in
> exploiting and aggravating the riots in Harlem, Watts,
> Cleveland and Chicago.[29]

Newsweek magazine was caught in a similar crossfire of
contradictory reports. On page 25 of the August 7, 1967
issue, the magazine quoted Justice Department officials "with

access to FBI intelligence data" as insisting that "there was no evidence of a conspiracy" in the riots. However, on page 13 of the same issue of *Newsweek*, FBI agents on the scene in Detroit were quoted as telling a different story. *Newsweek* said:

> The FBI men claim they spotted Negroes using walkie-talkie radios to report movements of policemen, firemen, and soldiers. Agents told Cyrus Vance, the President's able assistant in the crisis, that communications were precise enough to indicate previous drills and organization. FBI men made recordings and movies of ring leaders during the four-day rioting.

Rather than directly face the problem of communist agitation of racial disorders in America's cities, President Johnson and his administration asked Congress for billions of dollars to bolster the war on poverty. Such spending was supposed to help eliminate the conditions in the slums which the communists (which supposedly don't exist) would exploit. Any merit such an approach might have had was cancelled out when communists and other agitators *were among those selected to administer the programs*. In effect, arsonists were hired to help fireproof the buildings they planned to burn! In 1964, for example, America's largest circulation newspaper, the *New York Daily News*, revealed that . . .

> . . . Mobilization For Youth, a war on poverty organization with millions of tax dollars to spend, had three dozen employees with current or past connections with the Communist Party and other subversive organizations, including a member of the Communist Party's State Committee in New York. With communists helping to call the shots tax dollars were spent to promote rent strikes (organized by a Communist), school boycotts, and to train 300 young hoodlums in the use of rifles.[30]

Even the ultra-liberal *New York Post* spoke out. It charged that the Mobilization For Youth Director, Carl Brager, had turned . . .

> . . . fulltime paid agitators and organizers of extremist groups loose on the community to create disorder, disharmony, and violence — the very conditions MFY was created to combat.[31]

In March 1966, 50 New York policemen raided the headquarters of the Black Arts Repetory Theatre which had received more than $100,000 in federal antipoverty funds. In the building, policy discovered a rifle range and a well-stocked arsenal of deadly weapons. The head of the project, playwright LeRoi Jones, said, "I don't see anything wrong with hating white people." Federal funds were used at the "theatre" for an eight week summer school where 400 Negro children were instructed in hard-core black nationalism.[32]

Poverty war director, Sargent Shriver (a Kennedy brother-in-law) conceded that the program was "crude and racist in character." Even so, LeRoi Jones was back on the payroll of one of Shriver's Office of Economic Opportunity organizations a year later. In 1967, poverty fighter Jones was convicted for illegal possession of weapons during the riot in Newark. Charles McCray, chief accountant for Newark's anti-poverty office, was convicted with Jones on the same charge.[33]

A "liberation school" where 10 and 11 year old Negro children were taught to hate whites was operated in Nashville, Tennessee with federal financing. Nashville Police Captain John Sorace told a Senate committee that the "school" operated on anti-poverty money with . . .

> . . . Fred H. Brooks as director. Fred Brooks is driving a station wagon leased with OEO funds. He started driving it right after the grant was made. Not only is he a member of SNCC (Student Non-Violent Coordinating Committee) but so are half the student aids. It is almost common knowledge in our community that SNCC members have received the funds to operate these "hate white" programs.[34]

Poverty officials in Nashville first denied, then confirmed Sorace's charge that federal grants had been made for the program. When contacted by the press for comment, poverty fighter Brooks said that the federal government . . .

> . . . can keep their funds — we're going to continue operating. I think Sorace is a racist. He should be killed. He no longer serves a function in society.[35]

J. Edgar Hoover has said that communists work to "undermine and destroy established authority and to incite Negro hostility toward law and order." This communist program is now being implemented with federal tax money.

The widely-read labor columnist Victor Riesel charged that poverty war offices are riddled with revolutionaries. In a column written for August 1967 publication Riesel said:

. . . the Office of Economic Opportunity (OEO) and thousands of its tiny — sometimes store front — headquarters are loaded with literature and promoters of street action. Some of the latter are of the New Left, the independent Maoists, the Trotskyites, the pro-Peking Progressive Labor Party "youth", and even Muscovite Communist Party activists. . . . these young revolutionaries . . . run the poverty program.[36]

Two weeks after Riesel made this charge, police in Kentucky charged three anti-poverty workers with sedition. They had been distributing *The Communist Manifesto* by Karl Marx and Lenin's *The Task of the Proletariat In Our Revolution*. Supplies of such subversive literature were siezed in the raid in which the poverty war workers were arrested.[37]

Commonwealth Attorney Thomas Ratliff said he would protest against the assignment of Appalachia Volunteers, VISTA Workers, and workers from other anti-poverty groups in the area who . . .

. . . use federal funds to support subversive activities in Appalachia.

The U.S. Supreme Court ordered Kentucky officials to free the poverty workers, ruling that the state had no authority to prosecute sedition cases. Bail for the three poverty workers had been posted by Carl Braden, a longtime communist.[38]

Communists and those with close connections with the communists hold high positions in poverty war organizations. For example:

West End Community Council of Louisville, Ky., of which Braden's wife was an incorporator, received $28,000 in federal funds. The incorporation papers listed the Braden home as headquarters for the group.[39]

Deputy Director Hal Witt of the United Planning Organization, the principal Washington, D.C. anti-poverty group, is a son of longtime Communist Nathan Witt. Witt's $21,000 a year salary is paid with federal funds.[40]

The Congressman who exposed Witt's background said that while Witt had never been charged with being a communist himself, he had a long record of support for left-wing causes and fronts. The situation in New York is even more fantastic:

Robert Schrank, an identified communist, is director of the Neighborhood Youth Corps in New York City. An assistant to New York Mayor John Lindsay explained that Schrank is no longer a communist, having dropped his party membership to take his anti-poverty job.[41]

After Schrank's background was exposed, New York mayor John Lindsay described him as a "distinguished public servant." Since then Schrank has been promoted to the No. 2 spot in New York's poverty war. Lindsay was a member of the Presidential Commission which couldn't find any evidence of communist influence behind the riots.

Communist use of anti-poverty funds to further the revolution in America is all *according to plan!* When Communist Party spokesman Henry Winston returned from a Moscow consultation, he was quoted by *U.S. NEWS & World Report* as saying:

Today the Economic Opportunity Act has already become the basis for organizing the slums and ghetto communities and it offers the point of departure for helping to rally the rank and file millions to a mass movement.[42]

The same issue of *U.S. News & World Report* quoted the young revolutionaries as planning to . . .

. . . latch onto the poverty war funds and use the money to stir trouble.

THE WORST IS YET TO COME

Thus far, the revolutionaries responsible for the riots in Watts, Harlem, Detroit, Newark and a hundred other cities have only been practicing. Although 150 people have been gunned down on America's streets, 2000 others injured, and a billion dollars worth of property burned and looted, the conspirators have carefully refrained from exposing their full power and capabilities.

Ultimately, the communists — using the revolutionary black nationalist dupes they've trained — plan to bring America to a standstill. They can do it by coordinating riots in major cities with sabotage of electric power distribution, gas mains and water supplies.

Communist plans for paralyzing U.S. cities have been exposed by Congressional committees — although few Americans take the warnings seriously. In 1956, for example, the

House Committee on Un-American Activities conducted an "Investigation of Communist Activities in the St. Louis, Mo. Area." One of the key witnesses was Thomas A. Younglove. Younglove had served as an undercover member of the Communist Party for nearly six years for the FBI.

Younglove testified of sabotage schools conducted for party members. He told of boasts by the Missouri Communist Party chairman that he could completely immobilize the city of St. Louis with just . . .

> . . . 5 or 6 highly trained, highly disciplined core party
> personnel placed . . . (in) utilities, transportation, distribu-
> tion and waterworks.[43]

Tom Younglove, the witness who disclosed these plans, knew what he was talking about. He had been trained in the use of explosives. He worked for the Laclede Gas Company. He was the strategically placed man the communists were counting on to sabotage the gas distribution system in St. Louis when the final showdown came. The hearings did not uncover whether the communists had been able to place the 5 or 6 other agents where needed to sabotage the waterworks, electrical distribution, communication and transportation facilities.

Some of the revolutionaries themselves admit that they have not yet demonstrated their full power. H. Rap Brown, in an article published in the French political weekly, *Nouvel Observateur*, said:

> We are inferior in number. Therefore we have chosen
> guerilla warfare as a solution which the situation imposes
> on us. We will concentrate on strategic points in the
> country — in the factories, the fields, and homes of whites.
> We can easily sabotage and destroy without ever firing a
> shot. We can, for example, destroy telephone lines, railways,
> airports, the electric and electronic installations. The life of
> every city in the U.S. depends on the electrical system. If
> it is paralyzed, so is the city. Thus, city by city, we will
> succeed in bringing America to its knees.[44]

How vulnerable are American cities to such sabotage? When one circuit breaker failed in a remote power station in Ontario, Canada all of New York and New England were blacked out for many hours. A rash of similar power failures, many of them unexplained, have affected other widespread areas of America since. Could someone be practicing?

MOST NEGROES LOYAL

No responsible person has ever charged that any sizeable group of Negroes are communists or communist sympathizers. As a group, Negroes are probably more loyal to America than are college professors, as an example. Only a relative handful of American Negroes have tossed firebombs, looted stores, or gunned down firemen as they fought to keep flames from destroying Negro homes.

When Cincinnati Police Chief Joseph Schott testified of the role Stokely Carmichael played in sparking racial violence in Cincinnati, he added that . . .

> . . . 95 percent of Cincinnati's Negroes are heartsick over these riots and feel their opportunities have been diminished by the violence.[45]

However, communists have never sought the support of the majority. Lenin came to power in Russia in 1917 with the help of several thousand followers. Castro started with a band of 80 cut-throats in the fall of 1956. Within two years his campaign of terror — against the peasants he was claiming to help — made him dictator of Cuba. Similarly, a small fanatical group of terrorists operating as snipers, firebombers, etc. can produce havoc in any major city.

Even before any major showdown comes in the United States, if the communists can create widespread turmoil, U.S. troops might have to be recalled from world trouble spots to keep order at home. This would effectively destroy America's ability to resist communist aggression.

Instead of warning Americans, black and white, of the danger, America's top officials are encouraging the revolutionary ferment. On August 3, 1965, at a time of great tension in the country, President Johnson greeted several thousand college students as "fellow revolutionaries." Vice President Humphrey further dignified revolution as a means of protesting grievances. He told a group of New Orleans slum dwellers that if he had to live in some of our cities that he also might . . .

> . . . lead a mighty good revolt.[46]

WHAT CAN BE DONE?

If the communist program of using racial disorders to destroy America's ability to resist is to be thwarted, there is much to be done — by government and by the individual. Here is a capsule program of citizen action:

First: Don't turn to hatred. As J. Edgar Hoover has warned many times:

> The net result of agitation and propaganda by Communist and other subversive and extremist elements has been to create a climate of conflict between the races in this country and to poison the atmosphere.[47]

Hate and bitterness between whites and colored make the task of solving real problems which do exist between the races more difficult. When men turn to hate, only the communists benefit.

Second: Just as Congress *must* stop the trade and aid to the communist countries which supply guns and bullets for Vietnam, so also must federal financing of those who foment the war in the streets be stopped. Any Congressman who continues to support federal financing of the agitators should be replaced. Needed welfare programs should be financed *and controlled* at the local level.

Third: All citizens have equal rights to *tax-supported* facilities. *Real* inequities in our society should be corrected, realizing that government cannot and should not do all things. The government with the power to do all things *for* men also has the power to do all things *to* men.

Remember also that as new demands are raised as the "price" for racial peace that J. Edgar Hoover has warned:

> As soon as one set of demands is met, the communists immediately propose new and stronger demands calculated to provoke a new controversy and to act as a new source of social friction and unrest. The substitution of fresh demands for those which have been satisfied or outmoded in one way or another continues in a never-ending cycle with the aim of gradually convincing the "masses" of the need for a revolutionary transformation of society.[48]

This does not mean that efforts to correct *real* injustices should be abandoned — but corrective measures do not in themselves immunize a city against revolution. Cities such as Detroit and Los Angeles which have had the most "liberal" attitude toward civil rights have been hardest hit by riots.

Fourth: Communist exploitation of Negroes and the civil rights movement must be exposed. Negroes and whites must be educated so they won't be duped into helping the communists destroy America's ability to resist.

Books such as *Road To Revolution* by Philip Abbot Luce, *Color, Communism, and Common Sense* by Manning Johnson, and *It's Very Simple* by Alan Stang should be distributed. Luce was a white liberal. Because of his concern for the Negro, he joined the communists thinking he could advance the cause of civil rights. Soon after he was handed a gun in New York Central Park and assigned to start riots and promote a revolution, he left the communists. Since then, Luce has worked to expose their exploitation of civil rights. The *Washington Evening Star* said of his book:

> It describes in great detail, and with thorough documentation, the plans for guerilla warfare in the streets of our cities already devised by domestic radicals.

Manning Johnson, author of *Color, Communism, and Common Sense*, was a Negro. He joined the Communist Party in the 1920's thinking they wanted to help his people. When Johnson became a member of the Party's national committee, he saw that the communists only want to use Negroes to further the revolution. He left the Party and wrote the book to expose communist efforts in the civil rights field.

Fifth: Support your local police. Determine whether they have authority to put down trouble when it starts. Have they been hamstrung by political restrictions as police in Detroit, Newark, and other cities have been? Expose communist efforts to undermine confidence in local police forces. J. Edgar Hoover has said:

> . . . for years it has been Communist policy to charge "police brutality" in a calculated campaign to discredit law enforcement and to accentuate racial issues. The riots and disorders of the past 3 years clearly highlight the success of this Communist smear campaign in popularizing the cry of "police brutality" to a point where it has been accepted by many individuals having no affiliation with or sympathy for the Communist movement.[49]

Even if all these suggestions were implemented and every *known* agitator locked up, America would still have riots. As long as the communists can find two dozen embittered malcontents in a city of one-million people (or import them) riots can be triggered. Once the trouble starts, man's sinful nature insures that it will spread. Louis Lomax's study of the Detroit riot emphasized this. Lomax told how trained revolutionaries broke open the stores, and then . . .

> . . . the human element began to play into the hands of the revolutionaries. . . . People came from miles away to haul off freezers, sofas, television sets, and clothing.
>
> . . . A Negro woman, on relief, set fire to a furniture store because she felt she would never be able to pay the bill she owed there. . . . "Yes," she said, "I burned that store down. That's one bill I'll never have to pay. I made sure the office and all the records went up in flames first!"[50]

Why have such conditions never triggered riots before? Irish, Italians, Germans, Jews, and Negroes have all lived in "ghettos" and suffered discrimination at one time or another without rioting. During the Depressions of the 1930's there was real poverty and hunger in America. The Communists then had 100,000 members working for revolution. Except for a few mass demonstrations in New York and other cities and a month long siege of Washington by "veterans" demanding a bonus, they had little success.[51] They never suceeded in triggering the mass violence, looting, burning, etc. that has ripped America since 1964. What's the difference between 1932 and 1968?

RESTRAINED BY FEAR OF JUDGMENT

There was no widespread rioting in the 1930's because men knew that government then would have dealt quickly and forcefully with looters and other lawbreakers. There was also a general acceptance by most men of a possibility that God would judge and punish sin. In a society where Christians regularly proclaim God's message of judgment, men think twice before carrying away goods which don't belong to them — even if someone else broke the store open and the police aren't watching.

During the 1930's Christians — black and white — and most churches and clergy were still faithful in proclaiming God's warning to the wicked. Wickedness was restrained and order was maintained even in a time of great national stress. It was this function of the Christian which Jesus described when He told His disciples:

> Ye are the salt of the earth: but if the salt have lost its savour, wherewith shall it be salted? It is thenceforth

good for nothing but to be cast out, and to be trodden under foot of men. (Matthew 5:13)

Salt has many uses. Almost everybody knows that when cooked into food — or sprinkled on it — salt brings out the very best of the food's own flavors. Without enough salt, a meal is flat and unappetizing. In the Lord's day, salt was used as a preservative or curing agent to retard spoilage in meat. Salt in an open wound is very irritating. And, finally, as every pretzel and potato chip lover knows, salt produces thirst. The Christian, as the salt of the earth, should have these same effects everyday, wherever he goes.

Christians who really live the Golden Rule (Luke 6:31) bring out the best in people around them. Greeting everyone with a smile, bending over backwards to help those in need, letting others go first, etc. is "catching." In these ways, the Christian is like the "salt" which brings out the best flavor in food.

Christians who let the Lord show in their lives hold back corruption and wickedness in society by their very presence. They are like the salt which when it permeates a ham cures it and keeps it from getting rotten. When Christians' lives *show* that Jesus Christ is dwelling in their hearts, those around them put restraints on their language, temper, aggressiveness, etc. just as they do in church on Sunday or when a preacher comes to visit.

It is by proclaiming God's message of judgment to come, however, that the Christian really restrains corruption. There is wickedness in society because man has a wicked, sinful heart. He must be reminded of it. In doing this job, the Christian is as irritating as salt is in an open wound. The Christian is charged with the job of warning the wicked. God told Ezekiel:

> Son of man, I have made thee a watchman unto the house of Israel: therefore, hear the word at my mouth, and give them warning from me. (Ezekiel 3:17)

The message God wants the Christian to proclaim warns all men that . . .

> . . . it is appointed unto men once to die, but after this the judgment . . . for all have sinned and come short of the glory of God . . . the wages of sin is death . . . the wicked shall be turned into Hell . . . (Hebrews 9:27; Romans 3:23, 6:23; Psalms 9:17)

When Christians proclaim this message of judgment, men put restraints on their naturally wicked desires. They think twice before breaking the laws of God or man. For this reason, down through the ages, wherever *true* Bible Christianity has flourished men have enjoyed a maximum of freedom and liberty. This is true even though real Christians have never been in a majority in any country (just as there is never more salt than meat). When America was founded as "One nation under God" less than 10 percent of the people went to church. However, those who did set the standards for the nation. The other 90% listened because they could sense the presence of God in the life of the Christian. Christians set the standards in that day because, even though they were in the minority, they took the offensive. They believed God's promise which says:

Resist the devil, and he will flee from you. (James 4:7)

Christians in that day did not hesitate to stand up for what they knew was right, in spite of opposition. They trusted in the promises of a God who says:

One man of you shall chase a thousand: for the Lord your God, he it is that fighteth for you, as he hath promised. (Joshua 23:10)

Today, Christians have defaulted. The compromisers, the fast buck artists, the Black Power bunch, and the *Playboy* magazine crowd set the standards for the community — and the nation.

If you are a Christian, do you regularly warn others of the judgment which all men must face? Does your presence put restraints on the wicked ways of those around you — or are you so much like them that they feel perfectly comfortable with you? Do you treat everyone you meet in a way that shows you have Jesus in your heart? Do you radiate a joy, patience, love, goodness, faith, etc. which gives others a "thirst" to have the peace with God which makes you different? Are you the salt of the earth? Fifteen years from now is anyone likely to remember you the way a former Air Force lieutenant vividly recalls the witness of a young man he met during the Korean War. He says . . .

. . . it happened the first evening after a bunch of us — all new trainees — moved in to a big open barracks at Keesler Air Force Base in Biloxi, Mississippi. A hush seemed to fall over the noisy barracks when we realized that one man had dropped to his knees, bowed his head, and said his prayers.

He got to his feet to find everyone looking at him. He squared his shoulders as if he was waiting for the first wise remark. No one said anything for a minute — and then a tough, normally foul-talking fellow said, "OK, buddy, you've taught us something." From that time on whenever the Christian fellow was around, the men watched their language and you didn't hear all the usual foul talk and dirty stories.

Because most Christians don't exert this influence on those around them — on the job, in school, and in the neighborhood — wickedness is taking over the world. Jesus warned of such a time, saying . . .

> . . . if the salt have lost its savour, wherewith shall it be salted? it is thenceforth good for nothing, but to be cast out and trodden under foot of men.

Because the salt has "lost its savour" Christians — and all of society — are in danger of being "trodden under foot" of mobs stirred up by those who are fomenting world-wide revolution.

Chapter III

The War in Vietnam—
Destroying America's
Will to Resist

> *And it shall be in that day, says the Lord, that
> the understanding and courage of the king shall
> fail, and also that of the princes.*
> — *Jeremiah 4:9 (Amplified)*

AS THE COMMUNISTS HAVE WORKED to destroy America's *ability* to resist their takeover of the world, they have also been trying to destroy the *will* of the American people to resist. The war in Vietnam is part of their effort. Washington's refusal to win the war helps the communists achieve their goal.

In March 1967, the Senate Preparedness Subcommittee warned that the Johnson Administration, by "overly restricting" military efforts to win the war in Vietnam, might be falling into this communist trap. The Senate report said that . . .

> . . . the enemy strategy is to engage us in a protracted war of attrition which will tax the patience and undermine the determination of the American people to resist, once the true cost in precious blood and treasure is fully realized.[1]

Several months earlier a member of the committee, Senator Stuart Symington (D-Mo) spent several weeks in Southeast Asia. He returned to tell the Senate that the Johnson Administration was placing . . .

> . . . abnormal and unprecedented political restrictions on the use of air power in the Vietnam war.[2]

Symington charged that the restrictions "unnecessarily cost American lives, aircraft, and the chance of permanent success in the war." He read statements made to him by American airmen to support the charges.

One pilot told Senator Symington of flying over barges loaded with trucks, ammunition, and oil which had been unloaded from Soviet ships. He was forbidden to attack this barge or the Soviet ship in the harbor. Later, he said, he would be required to risk his life and his airplane trying to destroy the trucks one at a time after they had been unloaded from the barge and were travelling down the Ho Chi Minh trail. The pilot asked Senator Symington:

> Is not a North Vietnamese barge loaded with weapons and ammunition a legitimate military target?[3]

Another pilot told the Senator that he was forbidden to attack and destroy Russian-built MIG-21 fighter planes on the ground at their base near Hanoi. However, he is allowed to fight back when the MIG's take to the air and attack him from the rear. Senator Symington said:

> American military men and civilians in Vietnam are baffled by their orders from Washington.[4]

Is it any wonder that American military men are "baffled?" They are sent to fight and die against the communist enemy — but are denied the right to protect themselves or harm the enemy, except under certain mysterious "no-win" guidelines established in Washington.

Washington keeps American military men from hitting the enemy with all they've got. The Pentagon also keeps the communists informed officially on which targets will be hit — and which are safe from American attack. In September 1967, for example, American fighter bombers attacked a communist facility *near* the port of Haiphong. Some newspapers interpreted the attack to mean that Defense Secretary McNamara's long-time ban on bombing of the port itself had been overruled.[5] Two days later Washington notified the North Vietnamese officially that this was not the case. The port at Haiphong was still safe from attack. The Associated Press reported from Washington:

> The Pentagon, in its eagerness to show that Secretary of Defense Robert S. McNamara was not overruled in recent war decisions, has given North Vietnam official word that port facilities of Haiphong are safe from attack at present.[6]

Because the communists get official word from Washington on which targets will be attacked — and which are safe — they have been able to concentrate their air defenses at the vulnerable sites. As a result air losses from ground fire in Vietnam have been extraordinarily high.

When American pilots overstep the bounds placed on them (intentionally or by accident) the United States *apologizes to the communist enemy!* On June 20, 1967, for example, the U.S. apologized because a Soviet ship was damaged in an American air attack. It was hit while delivering a cargo to the North Vietnamese port of Cam Pha. Associated Press reported the incident on June 29 saying that . . .

> After initially denying an attack on the Soviet vessel, the State Department acknowledged June 20 that 20-mm cannon fire directed against a North Vietnamese antiaircraft position at Cam Pha might have struck the (Soviet ship) Turkistan. *Regrets were expressed for the death of the crew member and damage to the ship, and assurances were given that every effort would be made to ensure that such incidents do not occur in the future.*[7] (Emphasis Added)

Is it any wonder that thousands of career officers and enlisted men — the backbone of U.S. military forces — are leaving the services in protest against high level orders which aid the enemy?

The dead too are crying out — even if most Americans won't!

When Lieutenant J. D. Hunter of Arlington, Virginia, was killed in Vietnam, President Johnson sent the boy's parents the usual letter of condolences. The father answered the President saying that his son had been proud to serve in the U.S. Army but had complained that he and his men were required to fight a "no-win" war. Mr. Hunter asked the President to give our fighting men an opportunity to win. The grieving father concluded:

> Anything short of a real victory will only mean to Mrs. Hunter and myself and to thousands of other fathers, mothers, wives, brothers and sisters that their loved ones are being sacrificed on an altar of political intrigue.[8]

The President didn't answer. Instead, Mr. Hunter's heart-felt plea to the President was shuffled to Assistant Secretary of Defense Phil Golding, who wrote:

> We are engaged in a limited war for limited objectives. Our military actions must be weighed against those limited objectives. Our bombing operations in the North are conducted within certain constraints because they are tied to

our limited political objectives in the South . . . we are not seeking to destroy the Government of North Vietnam.[9]

After receiving this official, top-level acknowledgment that victory was not the goal in Vietnam, the anguished father wrote a final letter to the Defense Department. He said:

> My son often told me that he and his men were being called upon to fight a "no-win" war. How right he was! The inference in your letter is clear that, because of our "limited political objectives" in Vietnam, our soldiers will be allowed to fight only a "no-win" war with one hand tied behind their backs. What a miserable way to fight a war! You say we are not seeking to destroy the Government of North Vietnam. If the North Vietnam government and its stooges are not our real enemy in South Vietnam, pray tell me, who is?[10]

No-win complaints from Army and Marine ground troops stem from official policies. Ground is taken from the enemy time and again at great cost — and then troops are withdrawn without being allowed to hold the position. For example, during Operation "Hickory One" between May 18-28, 1967, two divisions moved into an area south of the De-Militarized Zone which separates North and South Vietnam and totally cleared it of invading North Vietnamese. When the operation ended on May 28, rather than being allowed to keep the ground they had won, the Marine and Vietnamese divisions were ordered to march back to their original positions. John Randolph of the *Los Angeles Times* reported:

> At that time, Marine infantrymen, dubious about 119 Marine dead and 817 wounded, grumbled, "Those bastards will be back in here the minute we leave."[11]

They were correct. On July 2, a battalion of Marines sent into the same area were ambushed. Before the fighting was over, 93 more Marines were killed and 309 were wounded. Again the Marines were withdrawn. Three weeks later, another battalion was sent into the same area and had 23 men killed and 191 wounded. The *Los Angeles Times* said:

> It is this constant fighting and taking casualties for ground that is never held that lies behind the growing criticism of the official strategy.[12]

Vietnam is not the first place where America's soldiers have put their lives on the line — without being permitted to win.

Fifteen years before Senator Symington exposed the "no-win" policy in Vietnam another generation of Americans fought communism in Korea. They suffered under similar limitations on their right to defend themselves. After the war some of their commanders told Congress about Washington-imposed policies which cost American lives — and aided the communists in their day-to-day conduct of the war.[13] General Mark Clark testified:

> I was not allowed to bomb the numerous bridges across the Yalu River over which the enemy constantly poured his trucks, and his munitions, and his killers.

In Korea, the principal communist line of supply was the Yalu River bridges between Manchuria and North Korea. They were "off-limits" to American bombers by orders from Washington. In the Vietnam war, the lines of supply included the barges that carried trucks, guns, and killers from Soviet ships in the Haiphong Harbor to the Viet Cong who were killing American GI's. Those barges, important railroad centers, dock facilities, and key industrial plants were also "off-limits" on orders from Washington.

When Congress investigated the Korean stalemate, General George Stratemyer, Air Force commander in the Far East, told the lawmakers:

> You get in war to win it. You do not get in war to stand still and lose it and we were required to lose it. We were not permitted to win.[14]

Because America's fighting men were not permitted to win in Korea in 1950-53, another generation of Americans had to fight the same communist enemy in Vietnam 15 years later — under the same "no-win" conditions.

As the Senate Preparedness Subcommittee warned . . .

> . . . the enemy strategy is to engage us in a protracted war of attrition which will tax the patience and undermine the determination of the American people to resist, once the true cost in precious blood and treasure is fully realized.[15]

How soon will America lose its will to resist?

Disenchantment with the no-win war has already caused many Americans to say "let's pull out." Senator Symington concluded his plea for unrestricted bombing* by saying . . .

*Interestingly, Senator Symington had been the Secretary of the Air Force during the Korean War when Generals MacArthur and Clark were not allowed to bomb the Yalu River bridges over which communist supplies flowed.

. . . if the administration refuses to unleash air power it would be better to terminate hostilities rather than continue fighting on the ground of a one against one basis.[16]

Other lawmakers followed his lead. When Secretary of Defense McNamara refused to permit increased bombing, the Republican leader in the House of Representatives, Gerald Ford, once a vocal advocate of winning the war, said . . .

I agree with Senator Symington that . . . we might as well get out as quickly as we can; as best we can. [17]

If the Vietnam war is ended without victory either by pulling out or by some type of face-saving negotiated settlement, other generations of Americans will have to fight elsewhere in the world. Finally, the nation will get tired of continual wars of attrition and stop resisting. This is demonstrated by history. In 1953, Senator Robert A. Taft (R-Ohio) said prophetically that President Eisenhower's willingness to accept a negotiated settlement for the Korean War and a divided Korea would spark further wars by freeing the Chinese to attack anywhere in Southeast Asia. Within a year the communists had moved into what is now Vietnam.[18] Because of an unwillingness to face the problem 15 years ago, America has suffered more than 150,000 additional casualties in Vietnam.

However the Vietnam war may be resolved, the communists are already planning new wars, confident that eventually America will tire of resisting. In July 1966, an article by William Ryan, AP's top foreign news analyst, asked:

What happens after Vietnam? Will there be other "people's" wars to test the strength and resources of the United States?[19]

AP surveyed the world trouble spots and concluded that the communists were strong enough to foment new Vietnams in Thailand, Africa, the Middle East, and in Latin America at any time. The Associated Press article quoted the official Chinese Communist party newspaper, People's Daily, as saying that a series of wars like the one in Vietnam will force the United States to dissipate its power around the world, weaken our country and its economy and make us vulnerable to eventual takeover. The Chinese communist newspaper said:

If some of the world's people [by which the paper meant Communist revolutionaries] strike at its head and others at its feet, divided U.S. imperialism can be destroyed piece by piece.[20]

In May 1967, the foreign minister of communist China said:

> The world needs not just one Vietnam, but three or four, and we will get them — in Africa, Asia and Latin America.[21]

The communists are certain that Americans will tire of fighting one no-win war after another and will let them have the world a piece at a time.

HOW WE AID THEM

The Chinese communists openly advocate world revolution and destruction of the United States. Soviet leaders smile and talk of "peaceful coexistence." As a result, many Americans have been deceived into believing that there is a meaningful split between the two countries. In clinging to the blind hope that the Soviet Union is mellowing, they ignore its role as the arsenal of world communism.

Without the oil, guns, bullets, grenades, food, fertilizer, jet airplanes and surface-to-air missiles supplied by the Soviet Union and her eastern European satellites there would have been no Korean War, no war in Vietnam, no rockets for Castro. Yet, most Americans have been led to believe that China is the real threat. China talks a tough game in Southeast Asia and advocates new Vietnams on every continent, but it is the Soviet Union, Poland, Czechoslovakia, Hungary, Rumania, etc., (the mellowed communist countries) who quietly supply the munitions to keep the war going.

Even so, as Americans died in Vietnam, America's leaders in Washington increased America's trade with the Soviet Union and her satellites. The expanded U.S. program helps to build up the communist industrial machine which supplies 80% of the guns and bullets used against Americans in Vietnam.[22] It is all *according to plan*. Lenin said that when the final showdown came between communism and capitalism, the American capitalist would sell the communists the rope with which they would hang him. Lenin said that . . .

> . . . the "cultured" class of the capitalist countries of Western Europe and America, i.e., the ruling classes, the financial aristocracy, . . . and the idealistic democrats . . . will grant us credits which will fill the coffers of the Communist organizations in their countries, while they enlarge and improve our armaments industry by supplying all kinds of

wares, which we will need for future attacks on our suppliers.[23]

Lenin's dream is being fulfilled.

WHAT CAN BE DONE?

The communist program for destroying America's will to resist can be thwarted *only* by (1) moving for a quick and decisive military victory in Vietnam (and wherever the communists start new wars in the future), and (2) by cutting off all trade and aid to the communist nations of the world.

In March 1968, *Science and Mechanics* magazine interviewed 12 of the highest ranking retired military officers. The magazine reported that they could win the war in six weeks by (1) officially declaring war on North Vietnam (2) closing the communist supply port at Haiphong (3) invading North Vietnam (4) destroying all important targets in the north after warning civilians in target areas to flee.

This program would be preceded by warnings to Red China and the USSR that any attempt to aid North Vietnam would be interpreted as an act of war against the U.S.

Simultaneous economic sanctions against the USSR would so weaken the Soviet Union that it would not have the resources to arm its satellites for other brush fire wars against the west.

This is not idle speculation. Lenin said that the stupid capitalists would . . .

> . . . enlarge and improve our armaments industry by supplying all kinds of wares, *which we will need* for future attacks on our suppliers. (Emphasis added).

Shortly after Kosygin came to power he confirmed this need, telling the Central Committee of the Communist Party . . .

> . . . in thoroughly developing our country's machine building, we must make use of foreign technology.[24]

Secretary of State Dean Rusk admits that communism is an economic failure. In a major speech in 1964, he said:

> We view communism as a system incapable of satisfying basic human needs, as a system which will eventually be totally discredited in the minds of men everywhere . . .

Throughout the communist world the economic short-comings of communism are vividly manifest . . . failures in food production . . . (a) standard of living even lower than it was before . . . the Soviet rate of growth has dropped below that of the United States and Western Europe and far below that of Japan . . . The fact that communism is economically inefficient has become increasingly plain to most of the peoples of the world.[25]

Why then do we fear communism? More important, why does the U.S. regularly bail the communists out of their economic difficulties with aid and trade? Whenever the communists admit they are falling behind the west in a key area, the U.S. provides aid. For example, on February 24, 1965 the Soviet newspaper *Pravda* called for . . .

. . . importation by the Russians of large amounts of western computers and technical know-how to make up for a serious lag in certain aspects of Russian computer development.[26]

In less than a month, the U.S. Department of Commerce licensed exports of 41 shipments of electronic computer equipment to the communist countries of eastern Europe, despite their potential for bolstering the communist war machine. As one newspaper pointed out . . .

. . . Computers may be used interchangeably on weapons design and manufacture, other scientific and technological problem solving, and a vast number of non-military applications.[27]

This is not an isolated case. As American boys fought and died in Vietnam, the government in Washington arranged for American companies to sell the communist nations . . .

. . . radio communication equipment, rocket engines, synthetic rubber, synthetic fibers, containers for explosives, computers, nuclear radiation and detection devices, fertilizer, chemicals, combustion engines, industrial processing control instruments, and various other products which build their war potential.[28]

The United States also regularly helps the communists to keep up with the West technologically. For example:

Under the 1966 Cultural Exchange Agreement, Soviet scientific teams were given *the right* to visit and probe deeply into such highly technical and vital installations as telephone and electronic facilities, gas and water treatment plants, high voltage electrical power transmission facilities, metallurgical laboratories, and plants producing chemicals and agricultural machinery.[29]

To make it easier for Soviet scientists to evaluate certain U.S. Air Force research reports, they were printed with a Russian language summary included.[30]

Congressman Glen Lipscomb (R-Cal), who exposed the practice, called the inclusion of the Russian language summaries in reports paid for by American taxpayers "incredible but true!" American taxpayers have also paid the bill for special training of communist nuclear scientists in the United States. Under the headline, "Tax-Paid Spies?," the *Indianapolis News* said:

> Five scientists from Communist-ruled Poland will have their nuclear research studies in the United States subsidized by the tax-supported National Science Foundation.
> The NSF has offered each of them grants ranging from $14,760 to $16,160 to travel in the United States and engage in research concerning high energy physics. In this work, they would have access to the Atomic Energy Commission's Brookhaven and Argonne Laboratories.[31]

In commenting on the arrival of the first of the Polish nuclear scientist-spies, Congressman Richard Roudebush (R-Ind) said:

> Only this past weekend the Communist government of Poland announced a mammoth demonstration to show support of the Communist cause in Vietnam. It's an incredible situation when during a time of war our government admits scientists from a nation allied with our foe in Vietnam.[32]

Why do the Soviet Union — and its satellites — need this regular help? Because of propaganda about Soviet space triumphs and the "great industrial growth" few Americans realize that the USSR is one of the world's most backward nations. Congressman John Ashbrook (R-Ohio) put the relationship between the United States and the USSR into proper perspective when he said:

> In order to enjoy the glories of the present Soviet system, we would have to abandon three-fifths of our steel capacity, two-thirds of our petroleum production, 95 percent of our electric motor output, destroy two out of every three of our hydroelectric plants, and get along on a tenth of our present volume of natural gas.
> We would have to rip up 14 of every 15 miles of paved highways and two of every three miles of our mainline

railroad tracks. We would have to destroy 18 of every 20 cars and trucks . . . We would cut our living standard by three-fourths, destroy 40 million TV sets, nine out of every 10 telephones, and seven of every 10 houses; and then we would have to put about 60 million of our people back on the farm.[33]

The usually very liberal executive council of the AFL-CIO recognizes the fallacy of Americans helping to build up the communist industrial machine. Meeting in Miami, Florida in March 1965, the council said . . .

. . . The Communists seek U.S. trade only to help overcome the serious economic difficulties while continuing to build up their arsenal of nuclear weapons.

Such help by American and other business interests can only finance and facilitate further Soviet aggressions against the democracies . . .

American businessmen would be guilty of terrible shortsightedness if they were to provide the Kremlin, on a business with usual basis, the goods and technical know-how it needs so badly.[34]

The Johnson Administration which the AFL-CIO sent to Washington — and continues to support — has arranged, promoted and encouraged the trade with the enemy by American business. Washington will continue to do so until the people of America — and organizations like the AFL-CIO — stop electing Congressmen who favor aid and trade to the enemy.

Efforts to stop foreign aid to the communists have regularly been defeated in Congress. On November 8, 1967, Congressman H. R. Gross (R-Iowa) tried to amend the foreign aid bill to prohibit any aid to nations which trade with North Vietnam. Congress defeated the amendment by a vote of 200 to 196.[35]

THE PROBLEM

America needs to elect a Congress which will stop *all* aid and trade with the communist nations of the world. Once the U.S. gets its own house in order, the other free nations of the world should be given a choice of trading with the United States — or trading with the communists. The world is at war. In war, there is no middle ground. Those who are not for freedom and against communism are helping the communists to win the world.

WHAT SHOULD YOU DO?

The book, *None Dare Call It Treason*, outlined a program of education, organization, and political action to achieve victory over the communists — and those within the United States who aid the communists.[36] Summarized, it said:

INFORM YOURSELF about communist programs, methods and goals. Determine for yourself how well they are doing. How do *your* Congressman and Senators feel about aid and trade for the communists? *How do they vote on these issues?*

ALERT OTHERS to the danger and help them to educate themselves. Do they know how your representatives vote on key issues?

ORGANIZE your helpers and plan your action. Mere numbers alone are not enough. Join and support existing anti-communist, pro-American groups.

WORK POLITICALLY because a program for victory over communism cannot be achieved until Americans elect a President and a Congress with the will to win *and* the courage to "cleanse" the policy-making agencies of government of those who, for one reason or another, have aided the communists down through the years. To accomplish this, conservative Americans must make their voices heard in the political parties.

For years, conservatives have distributed literature, sponsored speakers, joined groups, passed petitions, and worked politically — and the world situation has gotten worse and worse. In 1964, over one-and-a-half million Americans — some of them awakened by reading *None Dare Call It Treason* — distributed millions of books and tens of millions of pieces of other literature. They sponsored TV programs and rang doorbells for their favorite candidate, all without success.

Why have conservatives failed in their efforts? It is *not* due only to overwhelming odds, biased newspapers, lack of good TV coverage, or inability to get their story to a sufficient number of people — although these are serious problems. Conservatives have failed because a vast majority of them have neglected their spiritual responsibilities. They have assumed that their own efforts could prevail over the opposition, since history and logic demonstrate the correctness of the conservative position. In other words — "good" should triumph over "evil." However, the Bible records that Jesus taught, ". . . render unto Caesar the things that are

Caesar's *and* to God the things that are God's." Most conservatives claim to believe in God and the Bible. Few have read and accepted the message it has for them. As a result they work in their own strength to solve the world's problems. They haven't succeeded. Jesus told why when He said:

> I am the vine, ye are the branches: He that abideth in me, and I in him, the same bringeth forth much fruit: *for without me ye can do nothing.* (John 15:5)

Men have been fighting communism, socialism, and political liberalism in their own strength. They have failed, because Jesus has said that without Him we can do *nothing.*

Conservatives and Christians need to inform themselves, educate others, organize for action and work politically — if communist plans to destroy America's will to resist are to be thwarted. All such anti-communist programs, however, will fail in the future as they have failed in the past — *unless they are implemented in the power of God.* As St. Paul said:

> . . . we wrestle not against flesh and blood, but against principalities, against the rulers of darkness of the world, against spiritual wickedness in high places.

> Wherefore take unto you the whole armour of God, that ye may be able to stand in the evil day, and having done all, to stand.

> . . . put ye on the Lord Jesus Christ, and make not provision for the flesh, to fulfill the lusts thereof . . . For the weapons of our warfare are not carnal, but mighty through God to the pulling down of strongholds . . . (Ephesians 6:12-13, Romans 13:14, II Corinthians 10:4)

Chapter IV

Why are America's Leaders Betraying Us?

> *For among my people are found wicked men;*
> *they lay wait, as he that setteth snares; they*
> *set a trap, they catch men . . . their houses*
> *(are) full of deceits; therefore they become*
> *great, and waxen rich.*
>
> — *Jeremiah 5:26-27*

WHY DO AMERICA'S LEADERS fight communism with one hand while aiding it with the other? Enough Americans have asked that question that Dean Rusk, Secretary of State under Presidents Kennedy and Johnson, tried to give an answer. In a speech entitled, "Why We Treat Different Communist Countries Differently," Rusk said:

> We are asked how we can object to other free countries selling goods to Cuba when we are willing to sell wheat to the Soviet Union. We are asked why we refuse to recognize Peiping when we recognize the Soviet Union. . . . We are asked why we enter into cultural exchange agreements, or a test ban treaty, with a government whose leader has continued to boast that he will "bury" us.
>
> If the communists as a group has as their aim the destruction of our way of life, how is it that we can treat one Communist country differently from another? And why do we enter into an agreement or understanding with a Communist government over one matter, while accepting the hard necessity of continued hostility and conflict over other matters?

In other words, "Why do we fight them with one hand and aid them with the other?" Rusk's 4000-word answer is summed up in a few sentences from this same speech:

> Within the Soviet bloc the Stalinist terror has been radically changed. And within the Soviet Union, as well as most of the smaller communist nations, there are signs, small but varied and persistent signs, of yearnings for

freedom . . . it is our policy to do what we can to encourage evolution in the Communist world toward national independence and open societies . . . to promote trends within the Communist world which lead away from imperialism, away from dictatorships — and toward independence and open societies with freely chosen governments, with which we can live in enduring friendship.[1]

The hope, as expressed by Rusk, is that communism will "evolve" and "mellow" if not threatened by the west. This was the theory upon which Franklin Roosevelt was induced to give Stalin's armies occupation rights and therefore working control over a dozen eastern European countries following the Yalta conference.

Stalin, of course, did not mellow nor grant the promised elections to the Balkan countries. Instead, the yoke of communist dictatorship was placed on them. Even so, the theory that communism will eventually "evolve" and "mellow" into some sort of "open society" with which we can live peaceably became the basis for American foreign policy in 1946. It has remained so as Dean Rusk's speech confirms.

Arthur Schlesinger, Jr., historian and special assistant to Presidents Kennedy and Johnson, was perhaps the first liberal spokesman to write about the "mellowing" theory for public consumption. Writing in the May-June issue of the *Partisan Review*, Schlesinger said:

> The United States must maintain a precarious balance between a complete readiness to repel Soviet aggression *beyond a certain limit* and complete determination to demonstrate within this limit no aggressive intentions toward the USSR. (Emphasis added)
>
> . . . Given sufficient time, the Soviet internal tempo will slow down. The ruling class will become less risk minded, more security minded. Greater vested interests will develop in the existing order. Russia itself will begin to fear the revolutionary tendencies which modern war trails in its wake. . . . At the same time, U.S. backing to the parties of the (Socialist) non-Communist left and U.S. support for vast programs of economic reconstruction may go far toward removing the conditions of want, hunger, and economic security which are constant invitations to Soviet expansion.[2]

Schlesinger was here advancing the theory on which American foreign policy has been based since. The dream has been that if communism is "contained" within its borders long enough it will eventually "mellow" and evolve and give up the goal of world domination — particularly if the communists see that the rest of the world is achieving Marx's goal of world socialism through peaceable means. Schlesinger asked:

> Can the United States conceive and initiate so subtle a policy? Though the secret has been kept pretty much from the readers of the liberal press, the State Department has been proceeding for some time somewhat along these lines. Both Byrnes and Marshall have perceived the need to be firm without making unlimited committments to an anti-Soviet crusade, to invoke power to counter power without engaging in senseless intimidation, to encourage the growth of the democratic left. The performance has often fallen below its conception but the direction has been correct. Men like Ben Cohen, Dean Acheson, and Charles Bohlen have tried to work out the details and whip up support for this admittedly risky policy.[3]

During the 20 years that this "admittedly risky program" of containment rather than victory has been the basis for American foreign policy, nearly 800-million people have gone behind the Iron and Bamboo Curtains. Over 75,000 Americans have died trying to "contain" communism while being forbidden to defeat it. In the face of this record of tragic failure, the State Department, by Dean Rusk's own admission, still clings to the blind hope that communism will mellow.

In fact, the man who claims to have been the architect of the policy of containing communism until it mellowed, now says that his dreams have been realized: that communism has mellowed. George Kennan, who has served as a U.S. ambassador in various communist capitals, testified before the Senate Foreign Relations Committee on January 30, 1967. Kennan reviewed his 40 years of experience as a professional diplomat dealing with communism. He recalled his role as architect of the "containment" policy after World War II and said the program was based on . . .

> . . . a confidence that the Soviet Union would undergo changes that would permit easier relations with Moscow.[4]

Kennan claimed that the early hopes for a "mellowing" in the Soviet Union have been realized. He said . . .

. . . these changes have come. They are, in my earnest opinion, of such a nature as to give us, for the first time since perhaps 1917, real and hopeful possibilities for the adjustment by peaceful means of our relations with certain of these communist countries, particularly the Soviet Union.[5]

As Kennan spoke, Soviet-supplied missiles, jet airplanes, machine guns, etc. were killing and wounding Americans at the rate of 1000 per week in Vietnam!

Two weeks before Kennan testified, President Johnson told Congress the same story. In the 1967 State of the Union message, Johnson said:

As the first postwar generation gives way to the second, we are in the midst of a great transition from narrow nationalism to international partnership; from the harsh spirit of the cold war to the hopeful spirit of common humanity on a troubled and threatened planet . . .

We are shaping a new future of enlarged partnership in nuclear affairs, in economic and technical cooperation, in political consultation, and in working together with the governments and people of Eastern Europe and the Soviet Union.[6]

After 20 years of such hopeful talk about "meaningful changes" in the Soviet Union, the communists still boldly hold to their goals of world domination. Their role in Vietnam says so. Their words say so. On June 25, 1967, President Johnson and Soviet Premier Alexi N. Kosygin met at Glassboro, N.J. for "peace talks." At the conclusion of their meeting, President Johnson told the press and the people of the world . . .

. . . it is fair to say the summit has made the world a little less dangerous . . . he (Kosygin) and I agreed we wanted a world of peace for our grandchildren.[7]

At the same time, the Communist Party of the Soviet Union was releasing its proclamation in Moscow commemorating the 50th Anniversary of the Russian Revolution. It said:

The experience of the 50 post revolution years has borne out the conclusion of revolutionary theory that capitalism is doomed . . .

Imperialism, notably U.S. imperialism, was and con-

tinues to be the main enemy of the National-Liberation
movements.

> The successes of socialism have consistently demonstrated
> that the working classes ultimate aims can be achieved
> only thru a radical reorganization of society. At the same
> time history has proved the futility of the reformist way.[8]

In this statement, the communists announced to the world
that (1) they still plan to destroy capitalism and enslave
mankind (2) the United States is the main obstacle between
them and world domination, and (3) communism *must* be
established by radical revolutionary means rather than
through gradual reforms.

Tragically, America's leaders seem deaf to every such
Soviet reaffirmation of their dedication to the cause of world
revolution — just as they also seem blind to every evidence
in Vietnam and elsewhere that communism has neither been
"contained" nor "mellowed." Instead, they regularly insist
that "communism isn't all bad" — or if it was "all bad" that
it is now "changing." For example, when world leaders
gathered for the funeral of India's Premier Shastri in early
1966, Vice President Humphrey had a 90-minute conference
with Kosygin, who has just come to power in the Soviet
Union. On his return to the U.S. Humphrey gave the nation
a TV report on the conference. He described the Soviet
leader as . . .

> . . . frank, candid, polite, and reasonable.[9]

Humphrey said that he was convinced on the basis of
his talk with Kosygin that in years to come . . .

> . . . contacts between ourselves and the Soviet Union will
> expand and improve because of our mutual interests.[10]

Two days before Humphrey gave this reassuring report
to the American people on the *Face The Nation* TV program, Kosygin's government in Moscow announced stepped-
up shipments of arms and aid to Vietnam to repel the
"American aggressors."[11]

One week later, Averill Harriman finished a 22-day, 12
nation peace tour for President Johnson. TV newsmen asked
him how Soviet leaders felt about the war in Vietnam.
Harriman, supposedly the State Department's top expert on
the Kremlin, replied that the Russians are . . .

. . . embarassed by that war. They don't like it and they would like to see it stopped.[12]

If the Soviet leaders really want to end the war, why don't they stop shipping the guns, ammunition, missiles and MIG's to the North Vietnamese which keep the war going?

TITO AND FULBRIGHT

Leaders of Congress demonstrate the same blind refusal to see communists as enemies. On July 1, 1965, at the end of a 10-day state visit to Moscow, the Yugoslav dictator, Tito, joined with Soviet President Anastas I. Mikoyan in pledging "all necessary aid to North Vietnam."[13] Tito has also accused the U.S. of conducting a campaign of "mass murder" against civilians in Vietnam.[14] He regularly denounces America even though he has received over $3-billion in American aid since the end of World War II. Even so, America's leaders refuse to recognize Tito's allegiance to the world communist movement.

Three weeks after Tito lined up openly with the Viet Cong in their fight against America, Senator William Fulbright, chairman of the Senate Foreign Relations Committee, made a major speech in which he announced that Yugoslavia is . . .

> . . . a nation which is for most important purposes friendly, and certainly not hostile, toward the United States . . .
> On the whole their policies neither harm their neighbors nor threaten American interests. . . . it (Yugoslavia) has proven itself a reliable and stalwart associate in the advancement of certain interests on which our interests coincide.[15]

Fullbright concluded with the statement that the Yugoslav experiment in nationalistic communism has . . .

> . . . brought it to a position approximating genuine neutrality in the cold war.

Tito might be "neutral" in the cold war in Senator Fulbright's eye — but three weeks earlier he made it plain that he was on the communist side in the hot war in Vietnam.

The "blindness" with which Senator Fulbright is afflicted permeates the whole bureaucracy in Washington. Within six months after Tito had publicly lined up with the Viet Cong, the Johnson Administration . . .

. . . sold Tito 700,000 tons of American wheat, 92,000 bales of cotton, and 25,000 tons of food oil all on a ten-year easy credit payment plan.[16]

. . . loaned the Yugoslav dictator $175-million to shore up his economy and finance purchase of $40-million worth of industrial machinery and equipment including the communist nation's third nuclear reactor.[17]

. . . described U.S.-Yugoslav relations as the best in five years.[18]

Republicans show a similar blindness. After Dwight Eisenhower concluded his eight years in the White House, he was interviewed by the magazine, *U.S. News & World Report*. Eisenhower was asked his impressions of Nikita Khrushchev. The former president replied . . .

. . . Khrushchev is not another Hitler. Hitler was all black; Khruschev is not. The Russian has a sense of humor and gives all evidence of being a family man. He likes children and has a faculty for making them like him.[19]

Hitler was charged with killing 6-million people. Khrushchev, whether he likes children or not, was responsible for the deaths of over 10-million human beings. He was Stalin's chief hangman in the purge trials in 1936. He butchered Budapest in 1956.[20]

Why, then, couldn't Eisenhower see Khrushchev was every bit as evil as Hitler? Why does President Johnson talk of a "new partnership" and "economic and political cooperation with the Soviet Union" even as they step up shipments of arms being used to kill Americans? How can an experienced diplomat tell Congress that communism has been "contained" and that it has "mellowed" during years when the reds have enslaved 800-million people?

Are these men knowingly aiding the enemy? Are they misguided idealists? Can they be this stupid? It is hard to believe that influential men who have achieved success in every area of American life are totally devoid of intelligence. It is just as unrealistic to believe that *all* of America's leaders for the last 25 years have either been communists — or have knowingly been aiding the communists.

Some communists have undoubtedly reached top positions. Others have influenced the decision makers in government. Alger Hiss was at Yalta, working with Averill Harriman and Harry Hopkins, when Franklin Roosevelt was convinced that "Joe Stalin will mellow if you show him that he has nothing to fear from America."

That was nearly 25 years ago. How influential are communists in government today? It is impossible to know for certain[21] but there are some indications that the problem is serious. Elizabeth Bentley, a former communist, exposed two Soviet spy rings in which Alger Hiss, Harry Dexter White, Lauchlin Currie and about 80 others had participated. On May 29, 1952, she testified that at least two other Soviet spy rings were operating in the U.S. government. She had learned of their existence from her communist bosses, but she never found out who was in them, or in what branches of government they operated.[22] Whittaker Chambers, the man who exposed Alger Hiss, gave corraborating testimony.[23]

Neither of these groups have been exposed to this day! How influential have their members become in the last 16 years? It is impossible to tell. However, it took the Hiss-Ware group less than eight years to place members in top positions in every cabinet department after they came to work in government as young lawyers. They had placed at least one man in the White House as special assistant to President Roosevelt.[24]

Safeguards Congress established to prevent such a tragedy from happening again are being ignored or evaded within the State Department and White House. In 1961, the incoming Kennedy Administration appointed over 200 people to top jobs without obtaining the normal security checks and clearances. Walt Whitman Rostow, who had been denied a security clearance twice in the 1950's was among the 200. He was cleared on orders of Dean Rusk and Bobby Kennedy. By 1968, Rostow was serving as one of President Johnson's top advisers on Vietnam.

When Otto Otepka, a longtime State Department security official, told U.S. Senate investigators about the evasion of security safeguards, he was demoted. For six years, he has been fighting attempts by high State Department officials to drop him from government service.

As real as communist infiltration of America's government is, it is also unrealistic to believe that even a horde of communists could produce the emotionally-charged blindness which American leaders radiate when brought face-to-face with failures of America's foreign policy since 1945.*

Why are American's leaders so blind? Why are they betraying us? Man's answers to those questions are inadequate. However, God has an answer. In the Bible, God, speaking through the prophet Isaiah, warned His people of a time when He would take away the "wisdom of your wise men and the understanding of your prudent men." God said:

> Forasmuch as this people draw near me with their mouth, and with their lips do honour me, but have removed their heart far from me, and their fear toward me is taught by the precept of men: Therefore, behold, I will proceed to do a marvellous work among this people, even a marvellous work and a wonder: for the wisdom of their wise men shall perish, and the understanding of their prudent men shall be hid. (Isaiah 29:13-14)

God blinded the eyes of Israel's rulers. They tried to buy allies. They engaged in programs of aid to their enemies. They made pacts or alliances with the enemy. (Isaiah 30:1-7; Hosea 8:10, 12:1) They failed in most of the ways America's leaders are failing today. Their folly eventually took the

---

*Since the book, None Dare Call It Treason, was published I have had a number of confrontations with liberals — including some high-level ones.

In early 1964, Assistant Secretary of State Harlan Cleveland visited St. Louis to address a model United Nations meeting conducted by Missouri high school students. He appeared on a local Meet The Press-type show and I was on the panel. When we were introduced before the broadcast, he pulled himself up to his full 6'5" height, and asked, "Tell me — none dare call what treason?"

I replied, "Well, Mr. Cleveland, in the book I looked at the relative positions of the U.S. and Russia in 1945, the money and manpower we've spent opposing communism since then — the successes they've had in that time — and conclude that something is wrong with our foreign policy."

Cleveland is a handsome, distinguished man about 50 years old. When brought face-to-face with the failures of the postwar period, his pink cheeks turned red. His eyes got a stare in them. He clenched his fists and jumped up and down, saying in a strained voice, "I'll tell you where we were 20 years ago — we were at war — war — war! Now we have peace — peace — peace!" His face got even redder when he was asked where we had peace anytime since the end of World War II. The start of the TV show prevented him from answering. It's sobering to realize that a man as emotionally unstable as Cleveland appears to be, holds a top foreign policy position.

In March 1965, a chance meeting with Senator John Pastore (D-RI) on an early morning Chicago/Washington American Airlines flight produced a similar emotional reaction. I told the Senator I was troubled by the many contradictions in America's foreign policy. Pastore used the "mellowing" theory as the answer for every problem.

When finally forced to come face-to-face with the tragic results of 20 years of opposing communism with one hand while aiding it with the other, Pastore's final response was, "Young man, are you one of the people who want to blow up the world?"

Obviously scared to death at the thought of the mushroom cloud, Pastore seemed to fit the picture Alan Drury painted of the Senator in Advise and Consent who preferred crawling to Moscow on his knees rather than risk dying in freedom. Pastore, like so many liberals, clings desperately to the myth that communism will "mellow." This is how they avoid even thinking about a possible showdown with the Red Menace.

nation into captivity. God took away the wisdom and under-standing of Israel's wise men because the people honoured Him with words, rituals, tithes, sacrifices, legalistic obser-vance of the sabbath, etc. — but kept their hearts far from Him.

America is paying similar lip service to God. Our money carries the national motto "In God We Trust" but the Supreme Court has banned prayer and Bible reading from America's schools. In the pledge of allegiance to the flag, we still say we are "One nation under God." Rising crime, increasing rates of divorce, drug addiction, births to unmarried teen-agers, etc. make the words an empty slogan — lip service — rather than a reality.

How about you? Are you opposed to the Supreme Court decisions banning prayer and Bible reading from the schools? If so, do you gather your family to start each day with prayer and Bible reading? If such a practice is desirable for the schools, wouldn't it also be good for your family? Have you been guilty of paying lip service to God?

God dealt with Israel for this sin 2500 years ago. Would He deal with America today in the same way? Could these remote verses of Old Testament Scripture still apply? God anticipated that question. After speaking His warning, He told Isaiah:

> Now, go, and write it before them in a table, and note it in a book, that it may be for the time to come forever and ever. (Isaiah 30:8)

Why are America's leaders betraying us? Why do they seem unable to face the communist threat? Why do they fight communism one place in the world while aiding it everywhere else? God's Word has the only reasonable and responsible answer. Because men honor God with their lips . . .

> . . . the wisdom of their wise men shall perish, and the understanding of their prudent men shall be hid.

The Jews, to whom God directed this warning, paid lip service to the Messiah and King who was to come but when He came they rejected Him. The Scriptures say:

> He came unto his own, and his own received him not. But as many as received Him, to them gave he power to become the sons of God, even to them that believe on his name: which were born, not of blood, nor of the will

of the flesh, nor of the will of man, but of God. (John 1:11-13)

Many in America pay lip service to God today just as the Jews did 2000 years ago. They join a church. They've been baptized and confirmed. They send their children to church school. Many are leaders in the congregation and lead moral lives — but their hearts are far from God. They pay lip service to the Saviour who came 2000 years ago. They call themselves Christians but they've never let Christ come into their hearts to redeem them *personally* from their sins and give them a new nature. They are like Nicodemus, the ruler of the Jews who came to Jesus by night. He acknowledged Jesus, not as Saviour, Lord, and Master — but as a "teacher come from God." Jesus immediately admonished him, saying:

> Verily, verily, I say unto thee, Except a man be born again, he shall not see the Kingdom of God. (John 3:3)

Men today have religion — like Nicodemus did — but it is a religion of lip service. God commanded:

> Thou shalt love the Lord thy God with all thine heart, and with all thy soul, and with all thy might. (Deuteronomy 6:5)

How do you measure up against this commandment? God wants to be the all-consuming force in every life. Is He in yours? He can't be until you've been born again. Man, by nature, rebels against God. Adam and Eve rebelled against God in the Paradise He created for them in the Garden of Eden. The Jews rebelled against God in the Promised Land into which He lead them. Man today is in rebellion against God's rule over his life. That's why man needs a new nature and a new birth. To provide it, God sent His Son Jesus Christ to suffer the full punishment every man deserves. He then rose from the dead to be the new life of all who will believe upon Him and receive Him as Saviour, Lord, and Master. Anything less is lip service.

Why are America's leaders seemingly so blind to the threat of communism? God said:

> Forasmuch as this people draw near me with their mouth, and with their lips do honour me, but have removed their heart far from me . . . the wisdom of their wise men shall perish, and the understanding of their prudent men shall be hid.

God said it. Do you believe Him?

Chapter V

Communism, Youth, and the New Morality

> *. . . thy children have forsaken me, and sworn by them that are no gods: when I fed them to the full, they then committed adultery, and assembled themselves by troops in the harlots' houses.*
> — *Jeremiah 5:7*

THE COMMUNISTS who are working to make America rotten from within have as their prime target the Nation's youth. The first of the *Rules For Bringing About Revolution* published by the communists in 1919 says:

> Corrupt the young; get them away from religion. Get them interested in sex. Make them superficial. Destroy their ruggedness.[1]

What progress have the Reds made in getting American young people away from religion and corrupting them so they will not resist an eventual communist takeover? John Lennon, a member of the mop-headed Beatles singing group, says:

> Christianity will go. It will vanish and shrink. I needn't argue about that: I'm right, and I will be proved right. We're (the Beatles) more popular than Jesus now . . .[2]

Shortly thereafter, when the Beatles came to the United States, American young people helped to prove they were more popular than Jesus. In city after city crowds of up to 50,000 screaming teenagers paid $5, $10, and $15 per ticket (and sometimes sat in the rain) to hear the Beatles "sing." In an editorial entitled "Ships Without Compass," the *St. Louis Globe Democrat,* said there is "a spiritual vacuum" in America . . .

> . . . which has produced a crisis of "personal spiritual hollowness among students."[3]

The newspaper quoted the student body president at a large university as saying:

> At the heart of the students' problem is the lack of a meaning for living. Students have goals, but no purposes, plans, but no conviction that they are proceeding in the right direction . . . They even have causes; yet their lives are meaningless.[4]

In their search for reality, young people are trying revolution and rebellion, suicide, sex and psychiatry, drink, drugs, communism and crime. One leading religious magazine reported:

> Four thousand University of Colorado students — one-third of the student body — sought psychiatric help last year. Twenty-two students attempted suicide at another big eight campus; four succeeded. More than half of all college women have sexual relations before marriage, and one out of five is pregnant at the altar.[5]

The director of student health services at the University of California at Berkeley, Dr. Henry B. Bruyn, estimates that 25% of the students use marijuana and 10% have experimented with LSD.[6] On March 29, 1967, *The Crimson,* student newspaper at Harvard made similar estimates for that university. Police in Lafayette, Indiana confiscated marijuana plants which were being cultivated behind a fraternity house at Purdue University.[7] The president of the student body at Iowa State University resigned and dropped out of school because of controversy over his attendance at marijuana parties. He told newsmen:

> I can no longer take part in a society that condemns a man for having unpopular personal beliefs.[8]

Another student body president also dislikes American society but he didn't resign. Instead, he's advocating revolution. At a meeting of student "militants" in California, Devereaux Kennedy, 1967 student body president at Washington University in St. Louis, was quoted as calling for . . .

> . . . outright revolution and the overthrow of the United States government . . . terrorism on such a scale that it will demoralize and castrate America.[9]

Kennedy's was not an isolated voice. Dave Seeley of the University of California at Santa Barbara promised . . .

. . . the revolution is coming. We're bound to destroy the University — not by pulling it apart brick by brick, but we'll bring it to a complete standstill.[10]

In addition to proposals for future action, these youthful revolutionaries heard Stan Wise, secretary of the Student Non-Violent Coordinating Committee (SNCC), boast that his organization was . . .

. . . without doubt responsible for the race riots throughout the country.[11]

Is it any wonder that the chief theoretician of the Communist Party, U.S.A., Herbert Aptheker, has written:

This new generation is a beautiful one and is beginning to understand the need for basic structural changes in the United States.[12]

How are the Communists achieving their goal of corrupting America's youth and fomenting an atmosphere of revolution on the campuses? J. Edgar Hoover, writing in the February 1967 issue of the FBI *Law Enforcement Bulletin,* said:

. . . it is basic communist strategy to further communist objectives with non-communist hands, and this is exactly what is happening on some college campuses.

This was demonstrated at the University of California at Berkeley. Herbert Aptheker's daughter, Bettina, herself a proud, dedicated communist was elected to the important campus rules committee. The Associated Press reported:

The 21-year-old history major led all candidates for first place votes.[13]

Thousands of students on campuses across the nation have supported draftcard burning demonstrations and the "Vietnam Week" protests against U.S. involvement in Southeast Asia in April 1967 despite advance warnings by congressional committees that . . .

. . . planned student demonstrations against America's role in the Vietnam war have been promoted and are being organized by Communist Party leaders.[14]

THREE GOALS

The Communist attack directed at America's youth is designed to (1) split a few disgruntled, hate driven activists away from the mainstream of American life and train them as revolutionaries, (2) dupe as many non-communist youth as possible into supporting communist causes and programs, and (3) make the remainder of the nation's young people so corrupt and decadent that they will not resist an eventual takeover.

They are succeeding on college campuses — and in the nation's high schools as well. In December 1966, the New York City Board of Education announced plans to open . . .

> . . . two special centers for teen-age students who become pregnant. The centers would provide school classes, guidance and health services to girls who are now dropped from school during their pregnancies. Most of the girls are 15 and 16 years old, although some are younger, and the vast majority are unmarried.[15]

Similar centers were planned in St. Louis and other cities. School officials explain that the new service is necessary *because of a 39% increase in teen-age pregnancies in five years. The New York Times* said that school officials "had no explanation for the increase." Could the explanation be found in the words of the communists who ten years before said:

> Corrupt the young; get them away from religion. Get them interested in sex.

There are other tragic results from the sexual revolution in America. U.S. Public Health Service officials announced that by 1964 venereal diseases . . .

> . . . in the 15-19 year old group have increased 232 percent since 1957.[16]

By 1966 doctors in St. Louis reported that syphilis cases among teenagers in metropolitan St. Louis had increased 600% in the same period.[17]

TEEN-AGE DRINKING

Drinking by teenagers has also become a serious problem. A student columnist for a major newspaper reported:

> Teen-agers today are using alcohol — with and without parental approval — to an extent seldom recognized.[18]

To support his claim, the writer quoted a survey of 2000 high school juniors and seniors in which 19 out of 20 students questioned admitted that they had tasted alcoholic beverages at least once. One out of every four rated himself a "drinker," meaning that he drank more than just occasionally. A government sponsored study of the same problem found that one out of three teenagers are regular alcohol users. The average age at which students reported they started drinking was 14½. Some start a lot earlier — as this Associated Press report from Coos Bay, Oregon shows:

> School officials broke up a cocktail party at a playground and suspended 12 sixth graders, including three girls. Principal Kenneth Stocks . . . said the children mixed drinks taken from their parents' bottles at home.[19]

Drug use by highschoolers, while not as widespread as on college campuses, has many communities alarmed. In the prosperous Long Island community of Great Neck, New York a survey initiated by concerned high school students themselves showed that 10% of the student body had used marijuana and LSD.[20]

Smoking of marijuana among teenagers has increased so rapidly in New York's suburban Westchester County that Assistant District Attorney Thomas A. Facelle, Jr. said:

> It has become the way to gain social acceptance . . . The problem is staggering . . . youths in fine neighborhoods are getting big supplies somewhere and selling it to their friends.[21]

Walter Panas, a Westchester County school superintendent, said:

> Marijuana is a plague-like disease, slowly but surely strangling our young people.[22]

In metropolitan Boston, Wakefield school superintendent, Dr. Thomas D. Wade said:

> Any community that doesn't recognize that a lot of young people are dabbling with drugs probably has a real drug problem on its hands.[23]

The communists are deeply involved in the subversion of America's youth with dope. In 1961, the U.S. Commissioner of Narcotics Harry J. Anslinger told Congress that the communists were behind increased narcotics addiction in America.[24] Other enforcement agents testified of the part Castro's Cuba plays in flooding America with illegal dope. For the movie *Red China: Outlaw*, news commentator Lowell Thomas

interviewed Senator Thomas Dodd (D-Conn) about the
problem. Dodd pointed out the two goals the communists
have in selling dope. He said:

> Red China has peddled some 26-million pounds of illegal
> narcotics in the free world. She has raised more than a
> billion dollars in doing so . . . Red China has been peddling
> dope because she wants to undermine the people of the
> free world . . . She wants to destroy the minds and bodies
> and souls of human beings . . . to render them easy prey
> for subversion.

TEACHERS TERRORIZED

High schools are also in turmoil from a revolt against
established authority even more violent than that which is
manifesting itself on college campuses. In St. Louis, a Negro
leader who is also president of the St. Louis Board of
Education voiced concern that the rebellion has gotten so
bad that many high school teachers are afraid of their
students. He said:

> I know of many instances where teachers have been hit
> and threatened, where they've gone out after school and
> found their tires slashed. I doubt if you could find any
> who would talk about it . . . Teachers fear retaliation.
> Somewhere along the line, we in St. Louis and I guess
> the rest of the country have allowed young people to get
> too much out of control, to go too far.[25]

In Cincinnati, Ohio, police and school officials assigned
plain clothes patrolmen to school duty and established a
"buddy" system for teachers so they would not have to move
through school hallways alone.[26] In Chicago's suburbs, some
high schools racked by racial violence were kept open in
the fall of 1967 by armed sheriff's deputies and specially
hired guards who imposed "discipline rivalling a prison
camp."[27]

CHEATING AND CRIME

On June 16, 1966, the St. Louis Globe Democrat published
an editorial asking, are we becoming "A Nation of Bobby
Bakers?" The editorial was prompted by a Columbia University survey of 6000 students on 99 college campuses
which showed that at least half of the students "have engaged in some form of cheating." A similar survey done the

same year in an above average St. Louis suburban high school showed similar results — 54% of the high school students admitted they cheat in examinations. The newspaper said:

> Classroom cheating, taken increasingly for granted as a part of contemporary student culture, breeds a general disregard for moral values that carries over into other areas of living.
>
> Is it any wonder that cheating in all forms is rampant in our society from top to bottom? Is it any wonder that we have fixed contests and rigged quiz shows on radio and television, influence peddling in government, featherbedding in unions, fraudulent merchandising and tax cheating, padded expense accounts, lying by public officials, crime-coddling by the courts?
>
> By today's standards, too often the honest politician is one who, when he is bought, stays bought. Are we breeding a generation of Bobby Bakers and Bill Sol Estes?

As the newspaper pointed out, the moral decay which starts with classroom cheating can soon grow into other forms of thievery as a statement by the director of the student co-op at Yale University shows. C. L. Willoughby announced that shoplifting losses totalled $90,000 annually — an average of $15 shoplifting loss for each student and faculty member at Yale. He said:

> Mounting losses indicate a casual attitude toward petty thievery and a failure to understand the effect an arrest for stealing can have on a student's record.[28]

Other colleges report the same problems — and shoplifting losses in retail stores totals billions every year.

YOUTHFUL CRIME AND VIOLENCE

Since 1958, the crime rate in the United States has grown *five times faster than the population.*[29] In a speech in Chicago on November 24, 1964 J. Edgar Hoover said that . . .

> . . . this terrifying spiral in crime had come about through a growing wave of youthful criminality across the nation.

In testifying before the House Appropriations Subcommittee in February 1967, Mr. Hoover said that teenagers account for 49% of all arrests for . . .

> . . . the serious crimes of criminal homicide, forcible rape, robbery, aggravated assault, burglary, larceny and automobile theft.[30]

Much of the crime increase results from senseless violence from which the youthful criminal reaps little or no profit. A Pulitzer Prize winning reporter for the *Washington Evening Star* investigated activities of youth gangs in the nation's capital. He reported:

> The smashing and pilfering of stores is not part of some criminal conspiracy. There are no organized mobs intimidating customers and then guaranteeing store owners protection for a price . . .
>
> Instead, there is destruction for the sake of destruction, intimidation for the sake of intimidation, impromptu thefts and shakedowns, casually planned, quickly executed.[31]

Crime among young people is not limited to the center-city slums, the Negroes or the poor. It is rapidly becoming a major problem among the sons and daughters of the middle class and the well-to-do. J. Edgar Hoover has warned:

> In 1966, as during the past several years, the suburban areas, which are the cities and counties surrounding the large cities, reported the sharpest percentage of increase in the volume of crime.[32]

HOW HAS IT BEEN DONE?

The communists have had a lot of help in getting America's youth "away from religion" and "interested in sex." Decisions by the U.S. Supreme Court have removed prayer and Bible reading from America's public schools — ending the only contact some young people had with the Bible. On June 25, 1962, the same day it banned school prayers, the Supreme Court also opened the U.S. mails to a magazine published for homosexuals. The decision was one of a series under which such long-banned books as *Lady Chatterly's Lover* and *Tropic of Cancer* were classed as "literature" and were therefore exempted from obscenity laws.

As a result, U.S. Post Office officials estimate that $500,000,000 worth of mail order pornography — dirty books, postcards, and filthy magazines and movies — are merchandised to millions of youngsters every year.[33] FBI Chief J. Edgar Hoover has said . . .

> . . . it is a wholesale invasion of America's schoolyards and playgrounds.[34]

A group of four suburban newspapers in metropolitan St. Louis commissioned an investigation when an onslaught of filth hit the communities they served. The published report said of the "new" pornography:

> It's not the boy meets girl, boy catches girl, boy seduces girl type of sex story. Instead girl meets girl, boy meets boy, father meets daughter, and 15 boys meet one girl in teen-age sex orgies.
>
> It's being peddled by drugstores which sell paperback books. The pornography is displayed openly for all to see and buy. Merchants who sell the smut say they can't control what the distributor puts on their shelves — but strangely some stores which stock paperbacks have the dirty books and others do not.
>
> Once paperbacks which contained only mild or slightly suggestive passages were criticized for their lurid tempting covers. Now, the material available to your son or daughter brazenly promises lesbianism, homosexuality, sadism, wife swapping, incest and teen-age sex orgies on the cover and delivers it in bold detail on nearly every page.[35]

J. Edgar Hoover has warned repeatedly of the dangers from pornography. A particularly outspoken statement was included in the March 1968 *FBI Law Enforcement Bulletin.* Mr. Hoover said:

> The publication and sale of obscene material is big business in America today . . . It is impossible to estimate the amount of harm to impressionable teenagers and to assess the volume of sex crimes attributable to pornography, but its influence is extensive.
>
> Sexual violence is increasing at an alarming pace. Many parents are deeply concerned about conditions which involve young boys and girls in sex parties and illicit relations . . . Pornography in all its forms, is one major cause of sex crimes, sexual aberrations and perversions.

After surveying the influence of pornography, Mr. Hoover turned his attention on all phases of moral decay. He said:

> Is our society becoming so wicked that we are turning from virtue and integrity to immorality and degradation? Are we becoming morally bankrupt . . .
>
> Let us look about us. In the publishing, theatrical and entertainment fields, are the good, enlightening and educational qualities of their products being overshadowed by too much emphasis on obscenity, vulgarity, incest and homosexuality? Many people believe this to be true.

COMMUNISM AND PORNOGRAPHY

Where does such filth come from? Several State Legislatures and Congressional committees have disclosed that communists are using pornography as one of their many weapons to destroy American morals and "corrupt the youth." In September 1959, the Subcommittee on Postal Operations of the House of Representatives released a report on obscene publications. On page 14 the report said:

> The committee does not believe it unreasonable to suspect that there is a connection between pornographic literature and subversive elements in this country.

An investigation of communist activity in Great Britain made a similar observation about communist use of pornography to weaken the moral fiber of the west. The report said:

> This line of reasoning could be dismissed as the hysterical fears of the extreme Right, but for one or two documents which give chapter and verse of party instructions about the matter.[36]

The report cited a publication issued by the Italian Communist Party for its members in the movie industry which said:

> As a tactical policy, our aim is to defend an enterprise that is pornographic and entirely free of the restrictions of ordinary moral rules . . . that condone homosexuality . . . We are interested in encouraging this type of play, and we likewise are prepared to praise actors in such plays as champions of freedom . . . such bourgeois people, however cynical and contemptible they may be, are fighting on our side. They are in effect ants working voluntarily and without pay for us as they eat away the very roots of bourgeois society.[37]

In 1962, the Senate Armed Service Committee studied the sale of pornographic literature on military bases. It exposed the subtle communist propaganda interwoven with obscene material and disclosed that an important communist who died in East Berlin in 1959 had spent 27 years in the U.S. producing pornographic literature.[38]

In 1963, the Senate Internal Security Subcommittee investigated the operation of Castro's Fair Play For Cuba Committee in the U.S. It found that the first treasurer of this pro-Castro committee, Lyle Stuart, was also the publisher of a monthly magazine and books which had anti-religious, pro-Castro and unconventional sexual themes. Although never charged with being a communist, Stuart sat on the reviewing stand in Havana with the Castro brothers for a Mayday celebration.[39] In addition to pro-Castro books (including one authored by Fidel himself) Stuart's firm issued such titles as *Diary of a Nymph, Strange Lovers,* and *Pleasure Was My Business,* which claimed to be the personal memoirs of the operator of a house of prostitution.[40]

The chief counsel of the Senate Internal Security Subcommittee which conducted the investigation said:

> The committee has also been interested in the past and is interested now in what appears to be a repetitive connection between the Communist Party and purveyors of pornography.[41]

The "connection" goes back for many years. The "hero" of the much-banned *Lady Chatterly's Lover* was a communist organizer when the first edition was published. Later editions were revised to remove the open communist identification.

All pornographic literature is not the product of left-wing elements. Some of the smut is produced by fast-buck operators who want to get on the gravy train. The result is the same. Women's magazines which were once highly respected now glamourize and openly advocate premarital sexual relations and adultery. Church and government leaders respectibalize the breaking of the moral law. The Puritan Ethic is ridiculed and those who do become concerned about the moral decay among America's youth try to deal with the problem "rationally" without getting involved with "morality" or "God's Word." To effectively combat the corruption of America's youth it is important to understand the techniques being used and the influences they face.

EVERYONE'S DOING IT

Redbook magazine provides many illustrations. Once it was a respected women's journal. Now, it regularly features articles which promote the breakdown of morals. In September 1965, the cover feature was entitled, *How Successful Men and Women Arrange Their Married Lives.* The article was based on a "scientific" study which showed:

"Immoral" behavior, such as adultery, is amazingly common among successful Americans, but thoroughly concealed; almost all those who violate the accepted code of conduct live lives of pretense and apparent conformity.[42]

The theme is "everyone's doing it." The article doesn't say so, but the inference is "you are not among *the successful, the elite, the influentials,* if you are leading a chaste life."

This is not a new way to encourage immoral behavior. Teen-agers have always tried to evade parental restrictions with the plea, "But, mom, everyone else is allowed to . . ." Moses had the same problem. Shortly after he gave the children of Israel the Ten Commandments, he had to admonish them saying:

Thou shalt not follow a multitude to do evil. (Exodus 23:2)

NO PENALTY FOR SIN

Removal of the penalties for sin is another of the tactics used to promote moral decay and the "new morality." The *Redbook* article, for example, said:

Despite a general belief that "immorality" brings disaster, or at least enduring guilt, most of these non-conformists have suffered few or no observable ill effects from their behavior.[43]

To "prove" the point, the author presented numerous "case histories" of successful people living double lives in complete happiness. In fact, the only really unhappy person pictured in the whole article was a woman who bitterly admitted that she walked the straight and narrow. The wife of a "prominent doctor," she was quoted as saying:

So you're chaste before marriage, and what do you get? A reputation for being a cold fish, a string of "almost" love affairs, and a naivete that compromises your marriage almost from the start . . . Those girls of my college days who acted as if they didn't give a damn for reputation or marriage are now married, mostly to Ivy League men, and have children in high school or college. Oh, they've had their share of divorces and scandals and whatnot, but I'd trade my life for theirs in one second flat . . .[44]

The fear of pregnancy — another of "the wages of sin" which has tended to place some restraints on sexual promiscuity — has largely been eliminated by the "pill" which is being widely distributed to high school and college students today. For example, in April 1967, a Baltimore hospital announced that it . . .

> . . . provides birth control pills for the unmarried high school girl who is sexually involved with a number of boys or for the girl who is often intimate with her steady boy friend . . . Many of the girls are enrolled in the program by their parents and all must have parental consent to receive the pills.[45]

The same lessening of the penalties for sin is a factor in the growth of crime. *U.S. News & World Report* in its March 22, 1965 issue pointed out that while crime rates continue to increase . . .

> . . . the Supreme Court and lesser tribunals are grinding out decisions which stress suspects' rights — making it easier than ever for criminals to evade detection and punishment.

On June 13, 1966, the Supreme Court took a giant step in handcuffing law enforcement agencies. They banned the conviction of any criminal on the basis of his own voluntary confession *unless* he was given an opportunity to have an attorney present before talking to police.[46]

In the first 18 months after the Supreme Court handed down the precedent-breaking Miranda decision, over 100 self-confessed felons, including murderers and rapists were freed because of the high court's ruling. A typical case was described by this news story in the November 19, 1967 *St. Louis Post Dispatch.*

> BOISE CITY, OKLA — Nov. 18 — (UPI) A 14-year old boy who had admitted that he shot his mother 10 times with a rifle has been found not guilty of murder because he was not advised of his rights to a lawyer before he confessed to his father and two officers.
>
> The prosecutor assailed the acquittal as the "worst miscarriage of justice I've ever seen" . . . The judge said he based his "not guilty" ruling on a recent U.S. Supreme Court decision. He said he disagreed with the high court's ruling but that he had "no alternative."

Commenting on the new Supreme Court rulings, Frank G. Raichle, president of the American College of Trial Lawyers, said:

> It seems incongruous to me that under the present state of the law, a police officer may stop one while driving,

remove him from his automobile and then against his will take samples of his blood to see whether he has had a few beers, but yet may not ask him if he murdered his grandmother.[47]

The delinquent may get off easy if caught. Pregnancy and the social stigma resulting from an extra-marital relationship can be avoided. However, God's justice will have to be satisfied someday. His unchanging Word still decrees. . .

. . . the wages of sin is death . . . the wicked shall be turned into hell. (Romans 6:23; Psalms 9:17)

LEADERS SAY OK

Using "experts" from the field of education, the church, and government to justify or encourage moral decay is another of the techniques. In February 1967, for example, *Redbook's* cover article asked, "*Is Marriage Still Sacred? — The Explosive Debate That Is Disturbing Today's Clergy.*" For the most part the author presented the views of churchmen who are departing from Biblical positions on sex. Reverend Harry Williams, Dean of England's Trinity College was quoted as saying that . . .

. . . premarital or extramarital intercourse might be not only permissible but also a healing action in which Christ is present.[48]

The same blasphemous view was presented in the June 1967 *Playboy.* Nine clergymen — prominent in their denominations (Lutheran, Unitarian, Baptist, Presbyterian, United Church of Christ, Methodist, Episcopal, Catholic and Jewish) — were interviewed by *Playboy.* They generally agreed that where sex is concerned there are no hard and fast rules. Rev. Howard Moody of the United Church of Christ, said . . .

Are we able to say with dogmatic assurance that ALL extramarital sex is bad and destructive to the marriage relationship? As Reverend Adams indicates, most men engaged in counselling know that there are situations in which extramarital affairs have saved marriages, rather than destroyed them.

Young people don't have to read *Playboy* to get such advice. A conscientious high schooler in a south Florida city was deeply frustrated and bewildered as she sought answers for the problems of her life. The assistant pastor of her Methodist Church entertained the young people's group with cynical stories of how whiskey and women were smuggled into seminary dormitories. This troubled young lady cried . . .

> . . . even if it's true, why does he have to tell us? Why not give us something that will help us?

Even programs established to help young people have been used to corrupt them. President Johnson asked Congress to establish the federal Job Corps to train kids who drop out of school and retrain those who have had trouble with the law. The program was a massive flop. Job Corps camps became breeding grounds for dozens of riots and criminal activity which spread to nearby cities. Congressional investigators[49] disclosed these reasons why:

> A supervisor at the Casper, Wyoming Job Corps Center was hired by war-on-poverty officials in spite of 17 arrests for rape, assault and battery, and larceny.
>
> Among the first 16 Neighborhood Youth Corps leaders in Philadelphia, 13 had arrest records which included larceny, assault and battery, and morals charges involving minors.
>
> In Colorado Springs, five members of the city's anti-poverty governing board had police records. Their offenses included charges for sodomy, operation of a disorderly house, escape from a mental institution, burglary, and suspected of assault with intent to commit murder.
>
> Over 40 employees of the United Planning Organization which supervises the anti-poverty war in Washington, D.C. had criminal records. One of these ex-cons on the government payroll assaulted a young girl who came to his office looking for work.

Hiring of hardened criminals to "rehabilitate" boys who were in trouble was defended by government officials. When Congress and the press turned up dozens of cases of sex perverts and habitual criminals on the payroll of "war on poverty" organizations, James Kelleher, deputy director of public affairs for the government's Office of Economic Opportunity, said:

> It might be shocking to some people, but it's a plain fact that the tough youths will respect the former criminal.[50]

That, of course, was why they were in trouble in the first place. Washington's hiring of criminals to "rehabilitate" young hoodlums makes as much sense as giving aid to the communists with one hand while fighting them with the other — and has been just as unsuccessful.

Even parents get involved. In November 1967, *Redbook's* lead cover story was entitled, *"Sex Before Marriage: A Young Wife's Story"*. The author says:

> I feel premarital sexual experience in a stable relationship is healthy . . . I feel that young adult couples — and I stress adult — who have a healthy attitude toward sex can benefit greatly from a premarital relationship . . . I hope to bring my daughters up to share my ideas.[51]

These are examples of how church leaders, a young mother, and government programs have all dignified breaking the moral law and helped to implement the communist program of "corrupt the youth; get them away from religion. Get them interested in sex."

The warning of the prophet Isaiah still applies. He wrote:

> Woe unto them that call evil good, and good evil . . . the leaders of this people cause them to err; and they that are led of them are destroyed. (Isaiah 5:20, 9:16)

RIDICULE

The Puritan Ethic — which stems from a strict regard for God's revelation in matters of morals and religion — is attacked and ridiculed. An editorial column in the *Cleveland Plain Dealer* is a typical example. It defined a Puritan as one who . . .

> . . . lives in mortal terror that someone, somewhere, may be happy.[52]

Public officials who try to stem the tide of lawlessness and moral decay are subjected to similar ridicule and condemnation. Roger H. Harper is the state attorney in Broward County, Florida. After 30,000 college students spent Easter weekend in 1967 turning Ft. Lauderdale, Florida into a "20th Century Sodom and Gomorrah," Harper spoke out. He said the students:

> Plundered commercial vehicles, destroyed public property, burned a police patrol wagon, taunted and abused police, stole and ruined public property, explored illicit sex on the beach, dressed and conducted themselves salaciously and lewdly and overtaxed the city's courts and jails.[53]

The following day, Harper himself came under attack by government and business leaders in Ft. Lauderdale. Harper was said to show "an unfortunate attitude." A Ft. Lauderdale city commissioner said the throngs of students included . . .

. . . our future leaders. It's all a part of being young.[54]

King Solomon, the wisest man who ever lived, writing in Proverbs said:

> Withhold not correction from the child: for if thou beatest him with a rod, he shall not die. Thou shalt beat him with a rod, and shalt deliver his soul from hell . . . The rod and reproof give wisdom: but a child left to himself bringeth his mother to shame. (Proverbs 23:13-14; 29:15)

USE MAN'S WISDOM

When men do face the seriousness of the sexual revolution, they often try to deal with the problem "rationally" on the basis of man's wisdom rather than looking to God's law for answers. In the fall of 1967, for example, Fordham University, one of the nation's largest Roman Catholic schools, started a series of co-educational discussions on premarital intercourse, conception and birth control methods. Dean of Students Martin J. Meade said the issues would be discussed "frankly and directly" but . . .

. . . without touching on their morality.[55]

Man has always preferred to deal with moral problems without seeking what God has to say. If a group of people get together and decide what's "right" or "wise" the individual who differs can feel free to do as he pleases. However, there is no appeal from God's Word. This is not a new problem. When the children of Israel came to Mt. Sinai to hear God giving Moses the Ten Commandments they "removed and stood afar off and they said unto Moses . . .

. . . Speak thou with us, and we will hear: but let not God speak with us, lest we die. (Exodus 20:18-19)

The sinner doesn't want to hear God's Word for it brings him face-to-face with his guilt — and the punishment which he deserves. Adam and Eve were the first people to react this way. When they disobeyed God in the Garden of Eden, the Scriptures record that . . .

. . . they heard the voice of Lord God walking in the garden in the cool of the day: *and Adam and his wife hid themselves from the presence of the Lord God.* (Genesis 3:8)

HOW HAS IT BEEN DONE?

Religion and the Ten Commandments expose man's rebellious nature and place some restraints on it. For that reason, communists work to change or neutralize the teaching and authority of the church. Communists recognize that cutting man's ties to the Bible is the key to eventually corrupting and enslaving America's people. George Washington knew this too. He said:

> True religion affords government its surest support. The future of this nation depends on the Christian training of the youth. It is impossible to govern without the Bible.

For this reason, schools and textbooks of the colonial period were Bible oriented. For over 100 years first graders learned to read from the *New England Primer*.[56] It taught the ABC's this way:

A — In Adam's Fall, We Sinned All
B — Heaven To Find, The Bible Mind
C — Christ Crucify'd, For Sinners Dy'd

The McGuffey Reader series which replaced the *New England Primer* had a similar Biblical emphasis. The liberal historian, Henry Steele Commager, acknowledged this in an introduction he wrote for a re-issue of McGuffey's Fifth Reader. He said:

> What was the nature of the morality that permeated the (McGuffey) Readers? It was deeply religious, and . . . religion then meant a Protestant Christianity . . . close to Puritanism . . . The world of the McGuffeys was a world where no one questioned the truths of the Bible or their relevance to everyday conduct . . . The Readers, therefore, are filled with stories from the Bible, and tributes to its truth and beauty.[57]

That education and educators have different goals today showed when Commager wrote:

> That our children, today, are better taught than were their luckless predecessors is generally conceded, though we are sometimes puzzled that we have not produced a generation of statesmen as distinguished as the founding fathers.[58]

Even the best taught young people, by nature, rebel against the authority of God, country and family. They have a natural yearning for "forbidden fruit" — whether it be sex, drink or drugs. By exploiting these two basic weaknesses, the communists have had startling success since the restraints imposed by the widespread teaching of God's Laws in home, church, and school have been largely removed.

WHAT CAN YOU DO

Is there an answer? Shotgun marriages among teenagers, increased venereal disease, drug and alcohol use, and run-away crime rates all warn that the nation is dangerously close to becoming rotten to the core. Even if the present generation of Americans doesn't fall, what about the next one? Abraham Lincoln warned:

> The philosophy of the classroom is the philosophy of the government in the next generation.

In its editorial, *Ships Without Compass,* which discussed the moral vacuum in which young people are growing up, the *St. Louis Globe Democrat* said:

> A return to the ageless truths embodied in the Ten Commandments . . . is the only hope for a return to sanity.[59]

When man is brought face-to-face with the Ten Commandments, there are three results . . .

> . . . some restraints are placed on the natural appetite all men have for sin, (2) those who really try to keep God's laws find themselves sinners and guilty before God. They learn that man, by nature, cannot keep the Ten Commandments. Once a man realizes that he is guilty and deserving of punishment, he (3) sees his need for a Saviour to take his punishment. He sees his need for a new nature which is not in rebellion against God's laws.

The Scriptures teach that God gave man the Ten Commandments for these reasons. The Psalmist wrote that by "the law of the Lord . . . is thy servant warned." (Psalm 19:7, 11) St. Paul said God gave the Ten Commandments to show man his guilty, sinful state. He wrote:

> Now we know that what things soever the law saith, it saith to them who are under the law: that every mouth may be stopped, and all the world may become guilty before God.

Therefore by the deeds of the law there shall no flesh
be justified in his sight: for by the law is the knowledge
of sin. (Romans 3:19-20)

What happens once a person comes to see himself as a
sinner deserving of God's punishment? God deals with him
in a way which is very similar to the relationship of parents
to their children. Good parents usually establish rules for
keeping order in the home and insuring the safety of their
children. They prescribe certain punishments for breaking
the rules. God has done the same thing for the universe.

Most children, when they *get caught* breaking the rules
of the family, will invariably show great sorrow and beg
for forgiveness in an effort to escape the whipping they
deserve. Man does the same thing with God. Faced with
the repentant child, the wise parent will say, "Sure, son,
I'll forgive you — but first you have to take your punishment."
God deals with man the same way. Before forgiveness can
be granted, God's justice must be satisfied. God's only place
of punishment is in Hell. His punishment for sin is spiritual
death — eternal separation from Him in the torment of
Hell. What hope is there then for man — for all have sinned?

St. Paul gave the answer when he showed another of the
purposes of God's law. St. Paul said that the Ten Commandments,
by showing man that he is a guilty sinner deserving
of punishment, serve as . . .

. . . our schoolmaster to bring us unto Christ, that we
might be justified by faith. (Galatians 3:24)

The sinner who really believes that Christ suffered the
punishment due him personally can go to God and ask for
forgiveness on the basis that all the punishment for sin
has already been satisfied. The man who comes to God this
way gets forgiveness of sin — and a new nature as well.

This is the message that must be taken to the youth of
America — to the rebellious, drug-taking, sex crazy hippie
— and to the model young man and woman as well — for
the Scripture says . . .

. . . there is no difference: for all have sinned and come
short of the glory of God. (Romans 3:22-23)

Young America needs this message. So do many of their
parents. The communists have been working to corrupt the
youth for almost 50 years. Many corrupted "young people"

have grown up to raise families of their own. They are among the 80-million Americans who . . .

> . . . gamble away $50-billion a year and spend $13.5-billion on alcohol. They are among the 10-million Americans who are alcoholics, or problem drinkers on their way to becoming alcoholics. They are responsible for 1.1-million venereal disease cases, 250,000 babies born out of wedlock, and the 1.2-million abortions every year.[60]

This wicked generation needs to hear the warning of God's Ten Commandments. Even those who have never gambled, taken dope, or committed adultery need to hear God's warning — for all have sinned. Imagine for a moment that *you* are standing before God's judgment seat. The Scriptures picture that day. The Apostle John wrote:

> And I saw a great white throne, and him that sat on it, from whose face the earth and heaven fled away; and there was found no place for them.
> And I saw the dead, small and great, stand before God; and the books were opened: and another book was opened, which is the book of life: and the dead were judged out of those things which were written in the books, according to their works. (Revelation 20:11-12)

In that day, St. Paul says that you . . . "shall be judged by the law." (Romans 2:12) God said . . .

> . . . the word that I have spoken, the same shall judge him in the last day. (John 12:48)

God will look at your life — and test it against the perfection of His law. How will you measure up as He goes down the list of the Ten Commandments? Have you loved the Lord "with *all* your heart and soul and might?" No one has. Have you remembered "the sabbath day, to keep it holy" — *always?* No one has. Have you "honored your father and mother" *always?* No one has. Have you ever told one lie? *Even one?* Have you ever coveted something that belonged to someone else? *Everyone has.* In the day that your sins are exposed in the presence of an all Holy God, you will have no excuses, for . . .

> . . . every mouth will be stopped, and all the world will be found guilty before God. (Romans 3:19)

Actually, if you have broken even *one* of the Ten Commandments, you will be as guilty in God's eyes as if you broke them all. The Scripture says:

> For whosoever shall keep the whole law, and yet offend in one point, he is guilty of all. (James 2:10)

What happens once all men are found guilty? What about the punishment due for their sins? The Scripture describing the last great judgment says . . .

> . . . and they were judged every man according to their works . . . And whosoever was not found written in the book of life was cast into the lake of fire. (Revelation 20:13, 15)

Whose names are written in the "book of life?" Are those the "good" people? No — for "all have sinned." These are the names of the people Jesus died for — the names of those for whom He has already paid the price — the saved who have received the gift of eternal life from God.

On the basis of the sins you've already committed, you are guilty. Whether you will spend eternity in torment in the lake of fire will depend on whether or not you are one of the people Jesus died for. Are you? The Bible says if you are, you can and should know it. Are you one of the people Jesus died for? Scripture says:

> Christ Jesus came into the world to save sinners . . . (I Timothy 1:15)

Are you a sinner? If so, you qualify, for Jesus died for sinners. The Scriptures also say:

> . . . The Son of man is come to seek and save that which was lost. (Luke 19:10)

Are you lost and headed for Hell? If so, you qualify, for Jesus came to seek the lost. Jesus died for *lost* sinners. Jesus also died for the sheep. He said:

> I am the good shepherd: the good shepherd giveth his life for the sheep . . . I lay down my life for the sheep. (John 10:11, 15)

Are you one of the sheep Jesus died for? How can you know? He said:

> My sheep hear my voice, and I know them, and they follow me: And I give unto them eternal life; and they shall never perish, neither shall any man pluck them out of my hand . . . him that cometh to me I will in no wise cast out. (John 10:27-28; 6:37)

Are you one of His sheep? Are you one of the people Jesus died for? Have *you* ever come to Him asking for forgiveness of sins, believing that He died for you? If you have, He promises:

> . . . him that cometh to me I will in no wise cast out . . . Whosoever shall call upon the name of the Lord shall be saved. (Romans 10:13)

If you have never come to Him, his voice is calling you *now*. He says:

> Come unto me, all ye that labor and are heavy laden, and I will give you rest. (Matthew 10:28)

If you are one of the people Jesus died for, you will come to Him.

Chapter VI

The War in the Churches

*The prophets prophecy falsely, and the priests
bear rule by their means; and my people love
to have it so.* — Jeremiah 5:31

THE FIGHT AGAINST communism, J. Edgar Hoover
has said, ". . .is economic, social, psychological, diplomatic
and strategic — but above all it is spiritual."[1]

America is losing the economic, social, diplomatic and
strategic battles with communism because the traditional
spiritual leaders of the nation — the churches and the clergy
— are largely committed, knowingly or unknowingly, to the
communist side.

This is a serious charge — but careful investigation shows
that churches and men who call themselves "Christian" are
deeply divided today. The church is divided today over
such basic issues as . . .

> . . . whether or not America should resist communist
> attempts to impose its tyranny on such nations as Vietnam
> . . . the church and churchmen are divided over whether or
> not communism is good or evil and whether the church
> should promote or lead a war in the streets to achieve
> "social change."
>
> The church and churchmen are divided over whether or
> not God's laws against premarital sex still apply   . they are
> divided over whether or not there are any absolutes of
> right and wrong . . . and the church is divided, surprisingly
> enough, over whether or not God still exists!

To understand the seriousness of the problems, the positions taken by prominent churchmen — and church organizations must be examined carefully.

SHOULD WE OPPOSE COMMUNISM

American efforts to prevent communism from enslaving
the people of South Vietnam has been attacked and con-

demned by major church leaders and organizations. Since 1966, the World Council of Churches, of which most major U.S. Protestant denominations are a part, has regularly denounced American efforts to halt communism's spread. In February 1966, for example, the Central Committee of the World Council meeting in Geneva, Switzerland . . .

> . . . called upon the United States to halt its bombing of North Vietnam, pull its troops out of South Vietnam, and "review and modify" its policy of trying to contain communism.[2]

Such actions would permit a complete communist takeover of South Vietnam and the enslavement of its people. In July 1966, the World Council of Churches Conference on Church and Society condemned . . .

> . . . the massive U.S. military presence in Vietnam and the long continued bombing of villages in the South and targets a few miles from cities in the North.[3]

Delegates from Korea's churches tried to amend the resolution to include a similar condemnation of the communists. They were voted down 390 to 10. America's major churches (groups which are members of the National Council of Churches) had 73 delegates at the meeting. They refused to vote to condemn the communists — although they supported the resolution condemning the United States!

The World Council's general secretary, Eugene Carson Blake, is an American who served as Stated Clerk of the United Presbyterian Church in the U.S.A. for 15 years before taking the top WCC spot. In a speech at Norwalk, Conn. on April 29, 1967, Blake said . . .

> . . . religious leaders, with few exceptions, of all churches, cry out against what we are doing in Vietnam and warn us not to continue in that direction.[4]

The National Council of Churches and leaders of its member denominations have called for a halt in bombing and other actions to win the war and drive the communists out of South Vietnam. Such positions and actions stem from a deep division among churchmen over whether or not communism is good or evil. Over 30 years ago, the world famous Methodist missionary E. Stanley Jones, in his book, *The Choice Before Us*, wrote:

> When the western world was floundering in an unjust and competitive order, and the church was bound up with

it and was part of that order, God reached out and put His hand on the Russian communists to produce a more just order . . . communism is the only political theory that really holds the Christian position of the absolute equality of every individual.[5]

Since then influential churchmen have exhibited a similar tolerance toward communism. When 500 top leaders of America's Catholic, Protestant and Jewish churches gathered in Washington for a protest against America's policies in Vietnam, Dr. John C. Bennett, president of New York's influential Union Theological Seminary said . . .

> . . . the basic fallacy of U.S. policy in Asia is the axiom that communism is the worst fate that can ever come to any country.[6]

Bennett, a leading figure in the National and World Councils of Churches, expressed similar views in his book, *Foreign Policy in Christian Perspective*. In it, Bennett advocates a change in attitude toward China by the west. He displays a completely amoral attitude toward communism and the brutal revolution it brought to China in 1946-53. Read Dr. Bennett's condemnation of the American position on China, remembering that he is a top American religious leader. Bennett says:

> The American stance of moralistic hostility that seeks to keep China isolated from the international community is the worst possible approach to the problems which China raises. We should rather regard the Chinese revolution and all that has followed (the slaughter of 40-million human beings — Author) as a momentous human earthquake rather than as behavior to be judged by our usual moral yardsticks. It calls for awe initially rather than condemnation.[7]

Bennett calls for Americans to admire rather than condemn the Chinese communists. He continues:

> Communism has proved to be the instrument by which this nation has been united (by killing the opposition) . . . China has been able under communism to overcome the worst effects of its ancient poverty (food riots still rack China despite importation of massive amounts of wheat from Canada and Australia). Its women are full participants in national life (they have to leave their children and work like the men). . . .
> Say what you will about the cost of the revolution, the cost of allowing old social conditions to go unchanged

needs to be weighed over against it. Communism needs to be seen as the instrument of modernization, of national unity, of greater social welfare. The brainwashing, the cruel dealing with the opposition, and the political totalitarianism are the cost. At this stage, it is not for us to say whether we would or would not choose the effects at this cost.[8]

John C. Bennett is a leader in the World and National Councils of Churches. As head of an important seminary he is responsible for training young ministers. He frequently appears on television to give the "Christian" point of view on major issues. Yet, he cannot bring himself to condemn a Godless force which has brutally slaughtered 40-million Chinese. His words show that he is not a naive, uninformed man. He knows the communists used brainwashinging, mass murder, and dictatorship in bringing communism to China. Even so, he refuses to reject these "means" because they are being used to achieve what he believes is a good end.

Bennett is not alone in his views. The World Council of Churches Conference on the Church and Society heard Red China described as . . .

. . . the new saviour of the poor nations of the world.[9]

Similar views are expressed in Catholic circles. Msgr. Charles Owen Rice, in his column in the October 6, 1966 *Pittsburgh Catholic,* official publication of the diocese of Pittsburgh, Pa., used almost the same words as John C. Bennett. Msgr. Rice wrote:

> It may sound strange coming from a Catholic priest, but I am convinced we should pray for the survival of the present government of China . . . The present government, even though Communist, has brought order to its vast nation, order and admirable measures of internal justice and peace.
> Mao Tse-tung and his followers have changed China utterly, and the change has been for the better . . . To be sure he has established and maintained tight control, and has insisted on an austere program. He incessantly propagandizes. He, alas, uses hate as a weapon for control and motivation. Many are the mistakes of Mao and his coterie, but the evidence is that the men now ruling from Peking desire the welfare of the people of China . . .

While Msgr. Rice was writing these words Red Guards were roaming China carrying out a wave of terror in which at least five Catholic priests were buried alive and thousands of people were tortured and slain. His words reveal an ap-

parent awareness of such terror campaigns — and his approval
of them. He said . . .

> . . . terribly slow progress was badly dislocated by over
> communization and the Great Leap Forward. It is again,
> probably, being hampered by the current Red Guard
> campaign.
>
> However, that Red Guard campaign is not foolishness
> . . . The masses of China must sacrifice for the sake of the
> nation . . . Any development of a superior class to ride on
> the shoulders of the masses must be rooted out with
> periodic ruthlessness if Peking's program is to have any
> chance of success. Peking also must continue the virtually
> hopeless attempt to keep revolutionary fervor alive.
>
> We should look on this with a certain sympathy and
> tolerance . . . Actually we have to mix admiration with
> our sympathy for the miracle of management and mass
> manipulation that Peking has accomplished.

With men who think like John C. Bennett and Msgr.
Rice providing the leadership, the General Board of the
National Council of Churches voted 90 to 3 on February 23,
1966 to advocate admission of the Red Chinese butchers
to the United Nations.[10]

THE WAR IN THE STREETS

While church groups have increasingly been taking a
stronger pacifist stand against military action to halt communism, they have been in the forefront of those encouraging law breaking — and even violence — in support of "social
change." Associated Press reported that at the World Council
of Churches Conference on Church and Society . . .

> . . . a young American theologian created a stir by
> advocating violence for revolutionary groups such as the
> American civil rights movement.
>
> Richard Shaull, professor of ecumenics at Princeton Theo-
> logical Seminary, said this is sometimes the only way of
> achieving social change in the face of the self-satisfied,
> indifferent power structure of a contented society.[11]

A participant in the 1967 U.S. Conference on Church
and Society sponsored by the National Council of Churches
said the same thing. Rev. T. Richard Snyder, director of
church and community affairs for the Presbytery of Philadelphia, called for an "economic restructuring" of the United

States. Snyder refused to rule out the use of violence to bring about the economic revolution, saying:

> It is premature today for the church to make a decision about violence or non-violence for restructuring society. I'm not saying the church should take up bombs and grenades, but I don't think we can preclude this in the future, if all non-violent means prove ineffectual.[12]

Snyder was a part of the conference working group which studied the "Role Of Violence In Social Change." In their official report they concluded:

> One criterion for judging violence is whether or not the violence seeks to preserve privilege based on injustice or to redress wrongs. The former is unjustified violence. The latter can be justified.[13]

Individual churchmen have gone even farther. In a debate on Radio Station WOR, New York on August 10, 1967, the Director of Homeland Ministeries of The United Church of Christ, Dr. Willis E. Elliot, said that Negroes have made progress through . . .

> . . . nonviolence, threats of violence, and violence . . . Further progress will depend on the intelligent use of all three strategies, including strategic terrorism.[14]

Major denominations have passed resolutions approving and encouraging "civil disobedience" and "nonviolent resistance." In 1967, the Episcopalians lent their prestige — and money — to the Black Power movement. Before the church's general convention in Seattle, a group of Negro churchmen gave Presiding Bishop John Hines an ultimatum which stated:

> Black people are in revolt against an oppressive white society. We no longer will submit to rules designed to exploit us and propose to free ourselves by developing black economic and political power . . .
> Proclaim support of black power by committing, without strings, substantial money to black people for developing viable power bases.[15]

The General Convention of the Episcopal Church bowed to the demands and appropriated $3-million to support the black power movement.[16]

While admitting there was confusion over what "black power" means, the 179th General Assembly of the United Presbyterian Church in the U.S.A. meeting in Portland,

Oregon in May 1967 urged Presbyterians "not to be distracted by the controversy" over what black power means but rather to view it with understanding.

In his Yearend Report, J. Edgar Hoover warned that the increasing acceptance of the Black-power concept during 1967 has . . .

> . . . created a climate of unrest and has come to mean to many Negroes the "power" to riot, burn, loot, and kill.[17]

General church support and encouragement for "civil disobedience and nonviolent resistance" and a reluctance to define what "black power" means before supporting it, have provided the base and prestige on which Stokley Carmichael, H. Rap Brown, and other revolutionaries are building the "Black Power" movement which erupted into riots, murder, and mass bloodshed in the summer of 1967.

DIVIDED OVER RIGHT AND WRONG

Churches and churchmen are divided over whether communism is good or evil and whether violence can be used to achieve a "good" end. The division stems from a basic difference among churchmen as to whether or not there are any unchanging standards of right and wrong. John C. Bennett's amoral acceptance of the horrors communism brought to China is based on his relativistic view that there is absolutely nothing which is right or wrong in itself. Bennett rejects even the unchanging authority of the Scriptures. He told a meeting of the Associated Church Press that . . .

> . . . neither the Bible, or tradition, or theology provides a static authority for ethical questions.[18]

Bennett recommended that "Christian stands" on economic, social and political questions must be developed by a "consensus of churchmen from a wide variety of cultural and national backgrounds." In other words, when any issue arises, rather than looking to the unchanging authority of Scripture, Bennett suggests getting a group of clergymen together to decide what's best.

Other church leaders have similar views. Dr. Joseph F. Fletcher, professor of ethics at Cambridge Episcopal Theological School, favors amending the Ten Commandments to read:

Thou shalt not covet, ordinarily.
Thou shalt not kill, ordinarily.
Thou shalt not commit adultery, ordinarily.

"In other words," Fletcher says, "for me there are no rules — none at all . . . anything and everything is right or wrong according to the situation — what is wrong in some cases is right in others . . . a situationist would discard all absolutes except the one absolute: always to act with loving concern."[19]

A similar relativism is gaining acceptance in liberal Catholic circles. The 3rd Grade Teachers manual, for example, for the controversial new *Word and Worship* religion textbook series for Catholic schools advises . . .

> She (the teacher) should not hold up the observance of the Commandments as the ideal of Christian life . . . the teacher should not speak in terms of "You shall not" . . . The Christian is free from all such codes of law. (pg 68)

The 8th Grade Teacher is told:

> In the beginning the children will tend to judge things as black and white. Most have been taught that certain actions are sinful or not sinful. The teacher must try to help them see that the actions in themselves are in many cases indifferent. It is the intention and attitude of the person which really determine the moral character of the action. (pg 205)

CHURCH DIVIDED ON PREMARITAL SEX

With absolutes of right and wrong being discarded, a deep division has developed in the church over the relationship between the sexes — and those of the same sex. In the fall of 1964, for example, controversy erupted when the Episcopal chaplain of an all girls school in Baltimore, Maryland told his "congregation" . . .

> We all ought to relax and stop feeling guilty about our sexual activities, thoughts and desires. And I mean this, whether those thoughts are heterosexual, homosexual, or autosexual . . .
> Sex is fun . . . and this means there are no laws attached which you ought to do or not to do. There are no rules of the game, so to speak.
> And anyone who tells you that there are may be guilty of mistaking social and cultural custom for divine sanction or for what is sometimes called the natural law.[20]

The chaplain, Rev. Frederick C. Wood, Jr., tried to justify his advice by saying:

> The good news of the Gospel which has been delivered to me is that we have been freed from such laws as evaluative codes of behavior — freed to act responsibly according to a higher law.[21]

From his "sermon" it appeared that Wood's definition of this "higher law" would read, "If you love each other, anything goes." The Chaplain's superior, Bishop Harry Lee Doll of the Episcopal Diocese of Maryland, was interviewed by *Pageant* magazine about the sermon. He differed with some of Wood's conclusions but he agreed, "God does not say don't."[22]

This is not an isolated case. The United Campus Christian Fellowship is the joint campus movement of the Christian Churches (Disciples of Christ), Evangelical United Brethren, United Church of Christ and the United Presbyterian Church in the U.S.A. Four times a year it publishes a magazine called *Campus Encounter* for distribution on college campuses. An article, *Love Without Fear*, was included in Volume 3, Number 4 published in the winter of 1965. The author advocated (and described in detailed language which most postmasters would not accept for mailing) all types of sexual activity between old men and little boys, boys and girls and young adults. After picturing an "utopian" society where anything would go sexually, the author concluded:

> May I make it clear that I think these people would be free sexually in ways that are perhaps startling to us . . . it would be a love of bodies in all their different aspects . . . It would be bisexual in that there would not be the kind of fear that keeps two men from embracing and showing affection in this society . . . for in this age of nakedness and freedom there would be much self-confidence . . . It is a great and exciting challenge, something to aspire to and hope for . . . Someday perhaps we will know a few others — real people, whom we can love without fear and with whom we can become real.

The magazine which published this article was distributed on college campuses in the name of Christianity — using church funds!

Sunday school literature even in some supposedly conservative denominations has been infiltrated. *Baptist Young*

People, the official high school Sunday School quarterly of the South Baptist Convention, in its July-September 1964 issue recommended that the high school young people read the book, *Another Country,* by James Baldwin. This book is low grade filth and includes page after page of detailed descriptions of inter-racial sex play and intercourse.

Church literature and pronouncements of clergymen and churches show a growing tolerance of homosexuality. For example:

> In December 1967, Lewis I. Maddocks, an official of the United Church of Christ writing in *Social Action,* official publication of the church, recommended that the church "cease whatever discrimination exists against homosexuals, per se, in admission to seminaries, in ordination, and in employment of national denomination and local church staff."
>
> A conference of 90 Episcopal priests held by the Dioceses of New York, Connecticut, Long Island and Newark concluded that homosexual acts between consenting adults are "morally neutral." Such acts, they decided, should be judged individually on the basis of "whether the participants are expressing genuine love or are simply using each other for selfish purposes."[23]

These examples show that moral absolutes are being rejected. They are being replaced by the relativistic concept of 'if you love each other anything goes.' These changes are a reflection of the ideas advanced by a booklet published in 1961 for the United Christian Youth Movement by the National Council of Churches of Christ in the U.S.A. It was designed for young people looking for a guide to the relationship between the sexes. Entitled, *Called To Responsible Freedom, The Meaning Of Sex In The Christian Life,* the NCC booklet told these seeking young people . . .

> . . . For the Christian there are no laws, no rules, no regulations . . . Life is a series of grays and not pure blacks and whites.[24]

This position was justified by the National Council of Churches booklet on the basis that while in the Old Testament "adultery was strictly forbidden, as were other sexual deviations" . . .

> . . . both Jesus and the Apostle Paul were seeking to set men free from this sort of legalistic bondage.[25]

Whether the National Council of Churches knows it or

not, the New Testament also included many "laws" against sexual perversion, adultery, and fornication. St. Paul, for example, said:

> For this is the will of God, even your sanctification, that ye should abstain from fornication; that everyone of you should know how to possess his vessel in santification and honor . . . (I Thessalonians 4:3-4)

IS GOD DEAD?

Not only are churches and churchmen divided over whether communism is good or evil, whether there are absolute standards of right and wrong, and whether or not premarital sex is permitted by the Bible — but they are divided amazingly enough over whether or not God is dead!

Fewer than half a dozen young "theologians" have openly proclaimed, "God is dead." However, the National Council of Churches conducted a survey of the delegates and alternates who represented America's major denominations at its December 1966 General Assembly. The survey showed that one out of three could not attest to a firm belief in God — and only one out of four believe in such miracles as the Virgin Birth of Jesus Christ.[26] *These are the views of the leaders of major church denominations!*

The "God is dead" theologian has simply carried this unbelief and questioning of God's power to its logical conclusion. There is no such thing as "half a God." God is either all powerful and can do all things — or He is not God.

TROUBLE IN THE CHURCHES

The lead article in the April 18, 1966 issue of *U.S. News & World Report* asked the question, "Are The Churches In Trouble?" The magazine found that . .

> . . . all across the nation, religious unrest is becoming evident . . . Americans are suddenly waking to a big shift now taking place in their churches . . . They find clerics in the forefront of racial agitation . . . attacking U.S. policy in Vietnam . . . trying more and more to "involve" churches and synagogues in issues of the day.
>
> Back of the turmoil, churchmen find many disturbing signs . . . Despite rising membership, the proportion of Americans regularly attending church services declines steadily . . . Congregations are split on attempts to unify

churches and "modernize faith" . . . the number of young
persons studying to be ministers, priests and rabbis is
lagging behind population growth . . . and "millions of
dollars" have been diverted by unhappy laymen from church
funds and building and expansion programs.

The turmoil in the churches manifests itself in other ways
also. The attacks by church organizations on U.S. efforts to
halt the spread of communism and the inability of men
like Dr. John C. Bennett to see communism as total evil
has led to charges that there is communist infiltration or
communist influence in the churches. Such charges are regularly and vehemently denied and ridiculed by denominational
leaders and the National Council of Churches.* However,
a congressional committee investigated the charges and
reported:

> Thus far of the leadership of the National Council of
> Churches of Christ in America, we have found over 100
> persons in leadership capacity with either Communist-front
> records or records of service to communist causes. The
> aggregate affiliations of the leadership, instead of being in
> the hundreds as the chairman first indicated, is now,
> according to our latest count, into the thousands and we
> have yet to complete our check, which would certainly
> suggest, on the basis of the authoritative sources of this
> committee, that the statement that there is infiltration of
> fellow-travelers in churches and educational institutions is
> a complete understatement.[27]

Less than 5% of the clergymen in America have been
actively involved in supporting communist fronts and causes.
However, the ones who do are those who reach the top
positions in denominations, church councils, publishing
houses, seminaries, etc. They are also the vocal advocates
of abandoning absolute standards of right and wrong, etc.
For example:

In 1953, Herbert A. Philbrick, who served as an FBI
undercover agent in the Communist Party for nine years,
was asked by the House Committee on Un-American Activities to identify clergymen who regularly helped promote
Communist Party activities in Boston. Philbrick named
several and added:

---

*For a full discussion on how liberals try to misuse the words of J. Edgar
Hoover and FBI officials to avoid facing the danger of communist influence
in the church see None Dare Call It Treason, pages 132-34

The Reverend Joseph Fletcher, F-l-e-t-c-h-e-r, of the theological seminary, Episcopal Theological Seminary in Cambridge, Mass., is another. Joe Fletcher worked with us on Communist Party projects and an enormous number of tasks.[28]

This is the same "Joe Fletcher" who was quoted as advocating that the Ten Commandments should be changed to read:

> Thou shalt not covet, ordinarily.
> Thou shalt not kill, ordinarily.
> Thou shalt not commit adultery, ordinarily.

WHY ARE CHURCHES DIVIDED?

Why are churches and churchmen so divided? Why do men calling themselves Christians get involved with communists? Dr. John C. Bennett has written another book, *When Christians Make Political Decisions*, which provides a starting point for answering those questions. Bennett writes:

> Whatever the perplexities may be about the relationship of churches, of Christian teaching, of Christian citizens to politics, *there can be no doubt that we cannot separate our Christian faith from our political decisions as citizens.* (Emphasis added)[29]

Dr. Bennett says our political choices cannot be separated from our Christian faith. If this is so, then it is logical to conclude that since churches and churchmen are so divided politically there must be two different faiths or religions which both call themselves "Christian."

The Episcopal Bishop of South Florida Henry I. Louttit confirms this fact. In October 1964, Bishop Louttit's official diocesan paper, *The Palm Branch*, reviewed the book, *None Dare Call It Treason*. The reviewer discerned something in the book which few others realized. He saw something in the book which even the author did not realize when he wrote it. The review read:

> What does this book mean to Episcopalians? Speaking as it does, to warn people against communism and the dangers of infiltration of all our major institutions, it would appear, on the surface, to be an important book, particularly since it seems to be so well documented. *The fact that it is written from a definite religious point of view, as a basic premise, escapes many.* (Emphasis added.)

The fact that the author is not so much concerned about Communism, as he is about the religious conviction which colors all of his thinking, could easily be lost in his charges and insinuations against people and institutions whom he seeks to discredit.

John Stormer is a fundamentalist . . . *fundamentalists hold theological positions almost opposite, if not completely contrary, to the faith of the Episcopal Church and of every other major Christian body.*

This official Episcopal diocesan publication confirms that there are two different religions which call themselves "Christian." It also acknowledges that man's political differences are rooted in religious differences. The review spells out the fundamentalist theological positions which are "completely contrary to the faith of the Episcopal Church and of every other major Christian body." The article states:

The fundamentalists, John Stormer's ilk, hold the following positions: (1) They do not believe in the brotherhood of man. (2) They believe that individuals are saved through an individual religious experience. (3) They believe in the literal acceptance of every word of the Bible as the spoken word of God.

While apparently trying to portray Bible believers in a bad light, this reviewer has correctly drawn the lines between fundamentalists and theological liberals. Fundamentalists do not believe that all men are brothers — that lost people and born-again Christians are all children of God and therefore brothers "in Christ." Neither the Bible nor Jesus ever taught the "brotherhood of man." Jesus distinguished between born-again Christians (those who have become children of God by receiving Him) and unconverted people of whom He said: "ye are of your father the devil." (John 8:44)

Because lost people are children of the devil fundamentalists "believe that individuals must be saved through an individual religious experience." They believe it because Jesus Christ taught:

Except a man be born again, he cannot see the kingdom of God. (John 3:3)

Man is saved not through church membership, good works, baptism, or the sacraments, but by being born into the family of God through faith in the blood Jesus Christ shed on the Cross of Calvary for man's sins. Man sins personally. He needs a personal Saviour.

Finally, fundamentalists "believe in the literal acceptance of every word of the Bible as the spoken word of God." They believe it because the Bible itself claims:

> *All* scripture is given by inspiration of God, and is profitable for doctrine, for reproof, for correction, for instruction in righteousness . . . for the prophecy came not in old time by the will of man; but holy men of God spake as they were moved by the Holy Spirit. (II Timothy 3:16; II Peter 1:21)

If the Bible lies about itself and its origin, nothing else in it can be believed. So, fundamentalists accept "every word of the Bible as the spoken Word of God." The theological liberal, having rejected this premise (which this official Episcopal publication says every major Christian body has done) puts himself in the impossible position of having to pick and choose what he will or won't believe from the Bible.

Historically, the Episcopal Church "and every other major Christian body" held to these fundamentals which this liberal spokesman says they now reject. The 39 Articles of Religion of the Episcopal Church which every priest and bishop swear to believe and promise to uphold when they are ordained, teach that the Bible is the Word of God and that man must be saved through faith in Jesus Christ.

THE TWO RELIGIONS

All of men's political, social, and economic differences are, whether they realize it or not, based on spiritual differences. All men's spiritual differences stem from differing anwers to the question, "What is the nature of man?" Is man basically and inherently good — or is he basically selfish, self-seeking, self-centered, and sinful? How man looks at the Bible, Jesus Christ and man's need for salvation — in other words, his beliefs about religion — is determined by his belief about the nature of man.

There are just two religions in the world — they encompass all of the world's "religions," denominations, sects, creeds, etc. One of these "religions" teaches that man, being basically good, has the inherent capability or divine "spark" within himself to grow to become like God through self-denial and following the teachings and example of a divine teacher sent by God. Whether this divine teacher is named Jesus,

Buddha, Confucius or Mohammed makes little difference for their ethical teachings are essentially the same.

The other "religion" starts from the premise that man is by nature sinful and therefore incapable of pleasing God. It teaches that because of sin and rebellion against the God who made him, every man deserves to be punished and banned forever from the presence of the All Holy God. Because of his sinful nature, he is without hope except that God sent His Son to be punished in sinful man's place. This "religion" teaches that after the penalty for sin was paid, God raised His Son from the dead to be the new life and new nature of all those who will receive Him by faith as their Saviour.

If man is basically a sinner deserving punishment from God, it is essential that he places his faith, not in the example and teachings of Buddha, Mohammed, or even in a good man named Jesus — but in the sinless Son of God who died for man's sin and was raised from the dead to be the new life and new nature of those who believe. This is why Jesus said:

> I am the way, the truth and the life: *no man cometh unto the Father, but by me.* (John 14:6)

The Apostle Peter told the Sanhedrin:

> Neither is there salvation in any other: for there is none other name under heaven given among men, whereby we must be saved. (Acts 4:12)

This is why it is essential that every believer takes the good news of the Gospel to his fellow man. Apart from belief in the Gospel there is no salvation. This is why Jesus commanded:

> Go ye into all the world and preach the gospel to every creature. He that believeth and is baptized shall be saved; but he that believeth not shall be damned. (Mark 16:14-16)

RELIGION AND POLITICAL BELIEFS

Not only will man's religion be affected by what he believes about the nature of man, but his politics will be influenced as well. Man's position on the Constitution, free enterprise, communism and socialism, capital punishment, slum clearance and urban renewal, juvenile delinquency, premarital sex and the new morality, and almost every other political, social and economic problem will stem from whether he believes man is basically good or inherently sinful. How does it work?

RELIGION AND ECONOMICS

The success of pure socialism is predicated on the theory that if man is given the opportunity he will work to the utmost of his ability — and will only want to take for his labor that which he actually needs for himself and his family.

In theory then, in a socialist environment, a bachelor, a married man with two children, and a married man with nine children can all work side by side at the same job and the single man will be happy, if at the end of the week, he receives the $50 he needs to feed, clothe, and house himself while the man with a wife and two children takes home $125 and the man with ten mouths to feed receives a paycheck for $250.

Pure socialism has never worked anywhere in the world because it conflicts with the basic self-seeking nature of man. This is why the Soviet Union has never been able to feed its people — even though half of the total working force is assigned to the farms. In his book, *A Study of Communism,* J. Edgar Hoover described what happened when communism came to Russia. He wrote:

> By the spring of 1921 the Soviet Union under Communist rule was rapidly approaching economic collapse. The devastation of World War I, the civil war, the nationalization of industry by the Bolesheviks, and *the refusal of the peasants to produce more crops than they needed for their own use in protest against the Communist practice of requisitioning grain* all served to contribute to the chaotic economic situation. (Emphasis added)[30]

Man wants to personally reap the rewards of his own labors. That's why free enterprise, even with its shortcomings, works better than any other system. One American farmer, for example, outproduces 12 Soviet farm workers because he benefits personally from his increased productivity.[31]

Apologists for socialism like to blame climate, poor soil, and a variety of other factors for the poor showing of collectivized agriculture in the Soviet Union. However, their excuses are refuted by the excellent production achieved on the small amount of privately farmed land in Russia.

Each Russian family employed on a state farm is assigned one acre of ground to produce livestock, fruits and vegetables for their own use. They are permitted to sell what they don't need.

A recent study by *The London Observer* reveals how Russian farmland will produce *when the farmer can benefit from his labor*. The report showed that . . .

> . . . while "free enterprise plots" comprise only 3.7% of all the cultivated land in the Soviet Union, they produce 50% of all livestock, 65% of all fruit, 60% of all potatoes, and 45% of 11 other vegetables.[32]

Under free enterprise it is to man's advantage to produce as much as he can, as good as he can, as cheaply as he can. When he does, he'll be able, after selling the fruits of his own labors, to buy more of the goods and services of other men for the enjoyment of himself and his family. Thus, more people benefit more under free enterprise than under any other system ever devised. It works because free enterprise stems from a recognition that man is basically self-seeking.

SINFUL MAN AND THE WELFARE STATE

The men who founded and built America learned quickly that because man was by nature sinful and lazy that he would try to live off someone else's work and efforts — if he had the opportunity.

When the Pilgrims came to Plymouth Rock, for example, for several years all men worked fields which were held in common and all shared equally in the food which was produced. There was never enough food and many died of starvation. After three years of "welfare state socialism" the colonists made each man responsible for feeding his own family. An 1871 history text, *History of the World*, by Everet A. Duyckinck describes the results, saying . . .

> . . . the next year, because the joint stock system did not work well, each colonist at Plymouth began to plant a tract for himself, which soon made corn abundant.

A third grade history book, *Leaders In Making America*, published in 1921, tells how Captain John Smith dealt with the laziness which brought catastrophe and starvation to the colony at Jamestown. The text tells that Smith . . .

. . . laid down the law that "To save ourselves from starving, every man must turn to and help by working. He who will not work shall not eat." And every man had to obey the new rule. Although the lazy settlers did not like it, they set to work cutting down trees, building houses, clearing the land and planting corn. As we should expect, the outlook grew brighter. (pg 44)

As America has turned away from recognition of the sinful nature of man and his need of a Saviour, the welfare state has grown. Textbooks reflect the change. Few histories now teach the important lessons learned at Jamestown and Plymouth. Instead, they encourage the welfare state idea. Magruder's *American Government*, for example, teaches:

Because of sickness, accidents, and occasional unemployment it is difficult or impossible for a laborer who has reared a family to save from his meager wages. And it is more just to place all the burden of supporting those who have been unfortunate, *or even shiftless*, upon everybody instead of upon some dutiful son or daughter who is not responsible for the condition. (Emphasis added) (pg 339)

What is ahead? In 1966, a Columbia University sociology professor spearheaded formation of a union of welfare seekers which had the announced purpose of . . .

. . . combatting the Puritan Ethic that everyone in America has to work for a living.

This union in promoting the welfare state recognizes that it is revolting against Jesus Christ and His Word. The "Puritan Ethic" which taught that everyone in America had to work for a living — the rules that Captain John Smith instituted at Jamestown — came directly from the Bible which commands . . .

. . . if any would not work, neither should he eat. (II Thessalonians 3:10)

Why does man have to work? It is one of the temporal penalties for sin. Before God expelled Adam and Eve from the Garden of Eden for rebelling against Him, He told Adam:

In the sweat of thy face shalt thou eat bread, till thou return unto the ground; for out of it wast thou taken: for dust thou art, and unto dust thou shalt return. (Genesis 3:19)

THE CHRISTIAN AND FREE ENTERPRISE

The free enterprise system which stems from a recognition of the self-seeking nature of man also provides the best climate for the Christian. The born-again man with the new nature can go into the marketplace and sell his talents and products for the going price and use the proceeds to provide for his family, spread the Gospel and help other men as the Lord directs. St. Paul said:

> Let him that stole steal no more: but rather let him labour, working with his hands the thing which is good, that he may have to give to him that needeth. (Ephesians 4:26)

Because born-again Christians have too often failed to "give to him that needeth" — and do not care for the widows and orphans in the way the Scriptures command, politicians have the excuse they want to expand government programs.

THE CONSTITUTION AND SINFUL MAN

Our founding fathers were men who — from their study of history and/or because they had come to see themselves personally as sinners in need of the Saviour — recognized man's sinful, selfish, self-seeking nature. They had learned that down through history whenever man got power he used it to oppress other human beings.

Therefore, the men who wrote the U.S. Constitution tried to devise a system of government in which one self-seeking power hungry man would be pitted against other men who were also, potentially, self-seeking and power hungry. They theorized that if the powers of government were carefully divided among many men that each one, because of his nature, would jealously guard his own rights and perogatives and no one man would get enough power to become a tyrant or dictator. The history books describe this separation of powers between the executive, legislative, and judicial branches of government and the further separation between federal, state and local governments as a "checks and balances system."

The constitutional system of checks and balances has deteriorated in the last 50 years. As America had moved away from Jesus Christ and the related recognition that all men by nature are potential dictators, more and more power has been taken away from the states and the Congress.

In times of crisis and war power has been transferred to the president. Government textbooks acknowledge this trend — and the change in the thinking of Americans which has made it possible. Magruder's *American Government (1951)*, for example, under the heading, "Criticism of the Check and Balance System," says:

> The principle of checks and balances in government is not held in such high esteem today as it was a century ago. *The people no longer fear the officers whom they elect every few years.* (Emphasis added) pg 73

The people — and their preachers — no longer fear the officials they elect because they do not see themselves — and all men — as sinners needing a Saviour.

Man's approach to other major political, economic and social problems also grows out of his concept of the nature of man. For example.

> *Capital Punishment Controversy:* If a man murders his grandmother, with an axe, it must not be his fault if all men are basically good. Since some outside influence must have caused him to commit the crime it would not be just to execute him for it. This is the reasoning of churchmen and others who are agitating in many states to abolish the death penalty.

> *Slum Clearance and Urban Renewal:* If a man turns to a life of crime the fault must lie in his environment since he is basically good. Therefore the solution to the crime problem is to tear down the slums, remove the garbage from the streets, build public housing, etc. If, however, the trouble is in the man and not in his environment, he will create another slum in his new neighborhood unless his heart is changed.

COMMUNISM VS. CHRISTIANITY

Differences over the nature of man and how man's shortcomings are to be corrected is at the heart of the conflict between Bible Christianity and communism, socialism, and liberalism.

Karl Marx, the ideological father of communism, taught that man had no nature. He was simply matter in motion. Any good or evil seen in man was simply a reflection of his environment. Marx taught that capitalism was the cause of all the greed, selfishness, etc. in the world. He theorized that man would become perfect and an utopia would result if the evil in his environment (capitalism) could be eliminated and replaced by communism.

The teachings of Christ are in direct conflict with Marx's premise. Jesus taught that the evil of man originates, not from his environment, but from the heart. Jesus said:

> Do ye not perceive, that whatsoever thing from without entereth into the man, it cannot defile him . . . That which cometh out of the man, that defileth the man.
>
> For from within, out of the heart of men, proceed evil thoughts, adulteries, fornications, murders, thefts, covetousness, wickedness, deceit, lasciviousness, an evil eye, blasphemy, pride, foolishness: All these evil things come from within, and defile the man. (Mark 7:18, 20-23)

Man is influenced, of course, by his environment to the extent that he may change the image of himself which he permits the world to see. A desire for approval of family, friends, teachers, his employers, society — or the fear of punishment — may lead a man to place restraints on some of the wicked desires of his heart. However, he cannot change his own heart. The pressure to conform — and the standards to which he is expected to conform — vary in various areas of society. With a group of church people on Sunday morning, for example, man will try not to use the language which comes out of his heart all week. Men even try to clean up their lives to avoid looking at what they really are deep down inside — but it is to no avail — for the Scriptures tell us:

> All the ways of a man are clean in his own eyes; but the Lord weigheth the spirits . . . for the Lord seeth not as man seeth; for man looketh on the outward appearance, but the Lord looketh on the heart. (Proverbs 16:2, I Samuel 16:7)

What does God see when He looks into your heart? The Scriptures say:

> God looked down from heaven upon the children of men, to see if there were any that did understand, that did seek God. Everyone of them is gone back; they are altogether become filthy; there is none that doeth good, no, not one. (Psalm 53:2-3)

That is a blanket condemnation of the human race. It includes you. It includes the Psalmist David, a man who was mightily used of God. However, in the 51st Psalm David came face-to-face with his sinful nature. He cried out to God:

> Behold, I was shapen in iniquity, and in sin did my mother conceive me. (Psalm 51:5)

If you doubt that man is born with a sinful nature, ask yourself: Did you ever see a child who had to be taught to misbehave — or does it just come naturally?

Man is a sinner by nature. That's why every man needs a Saviour. That's why we need to be born again. That's why we need a new nature. This new nature is God's own Son who comes into our heart and becomes our new life — when we see our need and ask Him to be our Saviour, Lord and Master.

This is the historic Christian position. These are the glorious truths upon which John Wesley founded the *historic* Methodist Church. This is the teaching of the Westminster Confession which was the doctrinal standard of Presbyterian and Reformed Churches for 300 years. This is the truth found in the Articles of Religion of the Episcopal Church and the preaching of Augustine and Martin Luther. Most important, it is the message of Jesus Christ who taught:

> Except a man be born again, he cannot see the kingdom of God. (John 3:3)

St. Paul wrote:

> Therefore if any man be in Christ, he is a new creature: old things are passed away; behold, all things are become new; And all things are of God. (II Corinthians 5:17-18)

Tragically, the traditional message of Christianity "Ye must be born again" is not heard anymore in most churches which call themselves Christian.

WHY PREACHERS GO WRONG POLITICALLY

As the Bible shows the message of Christ cannot be reconciled to the teachings of Karl Marx because they start from completely different concepts of the nature of man. Why is it then that thousands of ministers who call themselves "Christian," have openly joined with the communists for joint action on certain projects and programs? Why is it that many more thousands of ministers who would never knowingly unite with a communist front regularly find themselves advocating the same solutions for almost every problem as the communists do? Why is it that churches which call themselves "Christian" no longer preach the message of Christ, "Ye must be born again"? The answer is to be found in the fact that political and religious liberals in the 20th Century have rejected the Scriptural view of man and his nature and have, knowingly or unknowingly, accepted most of Karl Marx's basic premises.

This is shown by a capsule summary of liberal philosophy written for the May-June 1947 *Partisan Review* by the historian and presidential adviser Arthur Schlesinger, Jr. Schlesinger said that liberalism . . .

> . . . dispensed with the absurd Christian myths of sin and damnation and believed that what shortcomings man might have were to be redeemed, not by Jesus on the Cross, but by the benevolent unfolding of history. Tolerance, free inquiry, and technology, operating in *the framework of human perfectibility*, would in the end create a heaven on earth, a goal accounted much more sensible and wholesome than a heaven in heaven.[33]

The liberal here rejects the sinful nature of man and the need for the new nature Jesus brings into the heart of a repentant sinner. Instead, the liberal looks for a utopia based on the hope that mankind can be perfected when science, education, and intellectual achievement changes his environment.

The religious liberal has adopted those same views on the basic goodness of man, his perfectibility, and the hope of creating a heaven on earth. Such thinking is reflected increasingly in official church literature, Sunday School materials, and the pronouncements of church leaders. For example, in the *Handbook for Christian Believers*, published by John Knox Press in 1964 and widely used in the Presbyterian Church, author A. J. Ungersma states that . . .

> . . . in the field of religion a school of thinkers today belittles man, his goodness, his powers, his significance.[34]

This "school of thinkers" base their views, of course, on the Scriptural concept of the sinful nature of man which Ungersma rejects when he says that . . .

> . . . man has infinite possibilities for growing to be more like God[35]

If man is basically good and has this capacity for becoming like God, then he doesn't need a Saviour. There would have been no need for God to come to earth in the person of Jesus Christ to suffer and die for man's sins. Ungersma takes this position and denies the Deity of Christ when he says . . .

In an honest effort to exalt Jesus, his followers sometimes have insisted that he is God. However, the Scriptures nowhere declare that Jesus made this claim.[36]

Jesus, of course, did claim to be God. That's why the Jews "took up stones again to stone him." Under the law of Moses, the penalty for blasphemy — for claiming to be God — was death by stoning. Time and again, Jesus said:

> I and my father are one . . . he that seeth me seeth him that sent me . . . he that hath seen me hath seen the Father; and how sayest thou then, Shew us the Father? (John 10:30, 12:45, 14:9)

In the 5th Chapter of John's Gospel, Jesus claimed for Himself all of the attributes of God. Even so, a columnist in *The Christian*, official organ of the Disciples of Christ in the November 26, 1961 issue stated:

> Disciples in general have never been able to accept the idea of Jesus being God.

Methodist Bishop Gerald Kennedy in his book, *God's Good News*, questions the Word of God and denies the Deity of Jesus Christ when he writes:

> I believe the testimony of the New Testament taken as a whole is against the diety of Jesus, although I think it bears overwhelming witness to the divinity of Christ.[37]

When Kennedy denies the "deity" but accepts the "divinity" of Jesus, he is lining up with such advocates of the "new theology" as Rudolf Bultmann of Germany and the late Paul Tillich in the United States. Louis Cassels, religion editor of the United Press characterized the "new theology" as teaching that God . . .

> . . . is revealed to men uniquely and supremely in the life of Jesus Christ. But this belief is often expressed in language which suggests that Jesus was a man who was so good and unselfish that God's love shone through his humanity, rather than in Biblical terms of the Word of God becoming flesh and dwelling among men.[38]

Each of these commentators, bishops and theologians seem to believe that Jesus Christ is not God come to earth to redeem sinful man — but rather that Christ was a man who became so good that he became like God. The implication is that by following his example and teachings, man today can do likewise.

The controversial new *Word and Worship* religion textbook series for Catholic grade schools conveys similar ideas.

A review of the series by the Cardinal Mindszenty Foundation,[39] a Catholic anti-communist organization, points out that the first grade teacher's manual directs the instructor to present Jesus . . .

> . . . as a Brother and Leader, rather than as the Son of God. The child is told first that he is "a man who loves children." The teacher is advised not to emphasize the power of Jesus or the miracles he worked.

Emphasizing the miracles Jesus did would point up His Deity. However, the second grade teacher's manual says the goal is to foster Christian attitudes so . . .

> . . . the child is not to look to Jesus as God, but as a man, and as a model for men.[40]

The third grade book pictures people who became "like Jesus" including a controversial French priest and the civil rights demonstrators, Martin Luther King and Mrs. Rosa Parks. Both King and Mrs. Parks are named ahead of Jesus in a list of brave "people." The 4th grade book includes Jesus in a list of men who became "famous" in various ways such as George Washington, Daniel Boone, and Babe Ruth.

NO HEAVEN OR HELL

Along with the denial of the sinful nature of man and his need for a Saviour, has come a downgrading or rejection of the hope of life after death in Heaven or Hell. In the Catholic textbook series which presents Jesus as "a model for men" the second grade teacher is told that . . .

> . . . in the past, Christians have erred by placing too much value on the soul and the world to come.

Bishop James Pike has been touring the nation assailing what he calls "this heaven and hell business."[41] He is not alone — although he is more outspoken than many who share his views. In March 1966, *The Milwaukee Journal* asked 275 Catholic and Protestant pastors in Milwaukee, "Do you believe that heaven and hell exist as actual places?"

Almost half (45%) of the Protestant pastors and over one-quarter of the Catholic priests could not say they believed in heaven and hell as actual places.[42] In the October-December 1966 *Crossroads,* the adult Sunday School quarterly of the United Presbyterian Church in the U.S.A., students were told . . .

> . . . Of course, we have to give up childish ideas about heaven as a place somewhere out there . . .[43]

A *New York Times* review of a new series of Catholic catechisms points out that . . .

> The whole question of hell and its supposed torments is passed over.[44]

A widely distributed official publication of the Methodist Church, a book called, *Basic Christian Beliefs*, teaches that the final book of the Bible with its detailed descriptions of heaven and hell is not . . .

> . . . to be taken as a description of events in heaven or hell, but as a vast, panoramic symbolic portrayal of what one seer (who, however, quoted others) thought the course of events here on earth was to be like.[45]

These examples show that like the political liberals described by Arthur Schlesinger, Jr. much of the church has adopted a religious liberalism which hopes to . . .

> . . . create a heaven on earth, a goal accounted much more sensible and wholesome than a heaven in heaven.[46]

The liberals have also abolished Hell. It is not needed. If man sins, it must not be his fault if he is basically good.* Therefore a just God couldn't punish him for it.

THE CHURCH AND ITS MISSION

Before He ascended into Heaven, Jesus Christ told His disciples:

> Go ye into all the world and preach the gospel to every creature. He that believeth and is baptized shall be saved; but he that believeth not shall be damned . . . teaching them to observe all things whatsoever I have commanded you. (Mark 16:15-16, Matthew 28:20)

Today, having decided that man is basically good and therefore not in need of a new birth and new nature, much of the church has turned its back on its great commission. They replaced it with a program of social action to change man's environment to create a heaven on earth. The Methodist Council on Evangelism at its November 1965 national meeting was told that . . .

---

*Six out of seven top church leaders in America reject the Bible teaching that man is born with a sinful nature, according to a survey by the National Council of Churches of delegates attending its 1966 General Assembly.

. . . seeking to save an individual soul is not evangelism and is not even Christian for these times . . . Old time revivals were proper for other times but it is not Christian for today.[47]

Ladies of the Methodist Church used the book, *Basic Christian Beliefs,* by Frederick C. Grant as the guide for their 1961 Lenten Bible study program. Published by the Women's Society of Christian Service, Board of Missions of the Methodist Church, it carried an introduction by Richard C. Raines who in 1967 completed a term of service as the Presiding Bishop of World Methodism. The author, Frederick C. Grant, was one of the translators of the Revised Standard Version of the Bible. He denies that Jesus Christ had to die for man's sins. He says:

To describe the death of Christ as a "propitiation" clearly implies an angry God who must be placated by the death of a sinless person: but this is not the meaning of the New Testament . . . Nowhere does Jesus suggest or even imply that divine forgiveness is conditioned upon his own death.[4]

Grant's statements are false. At best they demonstrate a lack of knowledge or understanding of the Scriptures. In the Gospel of St. John, Jesus Christ said:

I am the good shepherd: the good shepherd giveth his life for the sheep . . . and I lay down my life for the sheep. (John 10:11, 15)

Man is under a sentence of death for "the wages of sin is death." Jesus suffered this penalty as our substitute.

The same blasphemous denial that Christ died the death we deserve on the Cross of Calvary is found in contemporary Catholic literature as well. The new Catholic Encyclopedia denies the substitutionary death of Christ for us, although it admits that some Catholics have taught this doctrine in the past. This important Catholic reference work was produced under the sponsorship of the U.S. Catholic bishops. It carried the imprimatur of the Archbishop of Washington, D.C., Patrick A. O'Boyle. O'Boyle was promoted to the College of Cardinals by Pope Paul since the encyclopedia was published. The encyclopedia says:

Christ is never compared to the sin-laden scapegoat, or is the sacrifice of His life conceived as a punishment reserved for sinners to which he submits in their place (Vol 5, pg 760).

. . . vicarious expiation does not mean that Christ was punished in man's place (Vol 6, pg 761).

In contrast to this Catholic position, the Apostle Peter said:

For Christ also hath once suffered for sins, the just for the unjust, that he might bring us to God. (I Peter 3:16)

Even so, the Catholic Encyclopedia claims:

Christ, our Saviour, could never take the full punishment of sin upon Himself. He, the innocent, well-beloved Son of God, could never really be punished by His Father, not even as a substitute for all the brethren who would make one body with Him (Vol 12, pg 1096)

Contrast this statement with the Catholic Confraternity Edition of the Holy Bible. Isaiah 53:5-6, the prophecy of the coming Messiah, which was perfectly fulfilled in Jesus Christ, reads:

But he was pierced for our offenses, crushed for our sins; upon him was the chastisement that makes us whole, by his stripes, we were healed. We had all gone astray like sheep, each following his own way; but the Lord laid upon him the guilt of us all.

The literature of the World Council of Churches (WCC) also denies man's need to be born again and saved. *Study Encounter* is published four times a year by the WCC and distributed in three languages on college campuses and to Christian youth groups around the world. Volume 1, Number 2 was issued in the spring of 1965 and included an article on *"Conversion and Church Practices."* Based on a message delivered at a WCC Youth Conference, the article said:

Certainly in the Gospels one simply does not find a Jesus who is the first Evangelical Churchman! As a matter of fact, if it is the function of the preacher to "pluck brands from burning," one can only say that Jesus is rather irresponsible! When he confronts the crowds, he does not speak of their eternal destiny . . . He tells them how damn lucky they are to be alive and that there is no need to overdo it with their prayers! (Pg 102)

If you are a member of a church which is part of the National Council of Churches your money helped to pay to distribute this blasphemy on college campuses around the world. One wonders if this "preacher" has ever read the

New Testament words of Jesus Christ, The Evangelist, who said:

> For God sent not his Son into the world to condemn the world; but that the world through him might be saved. He that believeth on him is not condemned: but he that believeth not is condemned already, because he hath not believed in the name of the only begotten Son of God. (John 3:17-18)

> I say therefore unto you, that ye shall die in your sins: for if ye believe not that I am he, ye shall die in your sins. (John 8:24)

> Ye must be born again. (John 3:7)

This message is denied — or ignored — in the liberal church* today.

---

*It is also preached rarely in some churches, such as the Catholic, Lutheran, Episcopal and others, which believe that when a baby is baptized his sinful, Adamic nature is washed away and he is "born again." They believe that Jesus was referring to water baptism when he told Nicodemus, "Except a man be born of water and of the Spirit, he cannot enter into the Kingdom of God."

By comparing Scripture with Scripture, we see that this is not the case. Water here, as in many other places in Scripture, is symbolic of the Word of God. This is evident in Ephesians 5:25-26 where the Apostle Paul writes that "Christ also loved the church and gave himself for it, that he might sanctify and cleanse it with the washing of water by the word." The Apostle Peter confirms this in I Peter 1:23 when he writes: "Being born again, not of corruptible seed, but of incorruptible, by the word of God, which liveth and abideth forever."

It is the Word of God, applied to our hearts by the Holy Spirit, which shows us we are sinners, deserving of hell, and in need of the new birth. It is the same Word of God that gives us the faith (Romans 10:17) to trust that the blood Jesus Christ shed completely satisfies all punishment due for our sins. This is the faith which saves us and gives us the new birth. Once the Christian is saved, he should be baptized in water to show what has already happened to him.

The belief of the Catholic, Lutheran, Episcopal, etc., churches that regeneration (the new birth) comes at baptism is reflected in many other practices and customs of these churches.

For example, for about 1600 years certain designated portions of the Gospels and Epistles have been read each Sunday and Holy Day in Catholic Churches. These same Scripture selections are used in many Lutheran and Episcopal churches, the United Church of Christ, etc. They are selected largely from those parts of Scriptures written to instruct saved people on how to live because these churches teach that the people in their congregations were born again when they were baptized.

There are about 110 gospels and epistles in the 1967 Catholic missal. Of these, less than half a dozen even contain the word "saved" as it applies to everlasting life. In St. Paul's Epistles, for example, the early chapters are largely devoted to doctrinal teachings on man's sinful condition and God's provision for changing it — in other words, how to get saved. These are largely ignored by churches which teach baptismal regeneration. The later chapters in these epistles tell saved people how to live. These portions are read in these churches. As a result, many sincere church-goers regularly hear how they should live but are rarely if ever brought face-to-face with their need for a new birth and new nature to enable them to live the Christian life.

While Lutheran and Episcopal churches teach a form of baptismal regeneration, the more orthodox ones also emphasize that personal acceptance of Jesus Christ must follow for salvation.

Instead of challenging sinful men to repent and open their hearts so Jesus may live His life in a supernatural way in and through the body of the born-again person, the liberal preacher exhorts his listeners to live "like Christ." This is impossible for unregenerate man . . . "for all have sinned and come short of the glory of God."

HOW HAS IT HAPPENED?

How has this theological revolution been accomplished without the people in the pew coming to see what is being done with their church? Dr. John C. Bennett explains this also. Writing in the March 1966 issue of *Wind and Chaff*, published by the National Student Christian Federation, Bennett said:

> Churches often change convictions without formally renouncing views to which they were previously committed, and their theologians usually find ways of preserving continuity with the past through re-interpretations.

For a generation or more, churches have kept the old familiar terms while re-interpreting them, particularly for the children in the Sunday Schools. The process has gone far enough that there are few people left in the major denominations today with Biblical foundations for their beliefs. As a result when the final move is made to discard the creeds and doctrines upon which the church was founded and grew, there are few protests. In recent years, the United Presbyterian Church replaced the 300-year old Westminster Confession of Faith with a new, "modern" confession which pays lip service to the Bible as the Word of God, and then describes the Scriptures as . . .

> . . . the words of men, conditioned by the language, thought forms, and literary fashions of the places and times at which they were written.[49]

Denominational mergers have presented similar opportunities for church liberals to drop Biblical doctrines from church creeds. Most members don't notice because years of "re-interpreting" have left most of them fuzzy about what they believe. When the Evangelical and Reformed and Congregational-Christian Churches merged, for example, the proposed creed for the new United Church of Christ did not mention the Trinity nor did it affirm the Deity of Jesus Christ by calling Him God.[50]

WHAT SHOULD YOU DO?

If you are in a church which is part of the ecumenical movement and/or where you are not regularly and forcefully brought face-to-face with *your* need of salvation and the new birth, what should you do?

First, you must decide for yourself whether or not you've ever really been born again. Have you become "a new creature in Christ." If you haven't, or if you are not sure, you can be born again right now. Are you a sinner who deserves to go to hell? Do you believe that when Jesus Christ died, He suffered *all* the punishment due for your sins? Do you believe He was buried and then rose from the dead? If so, ask Him to forgive your sins and invite Him to come into your heart to be *your* Saviour, Lord and Master.

Once you've taken this step, trust God's promises which say:

> . . . him that cometh to me I will in no wise cast out . . . For whosoever shall call upon the name of the Lord *shall* be saved. (John 6:37, Romans 10:13)

Salvation is the result, not of feeling differently immediately — nor of seeing a starburst in the heavens — but of believing God's promises. This is faith — the "feeling" will come later.

Once you are a Christian the question, "What should I do?" becomes, "What would God have me to do about the church I am in?" His Word gives us the answer for every problem we face. In II Corinthians 6:14-7:1, God has the answer for those who are in churches which no longer believe or preach the Word of God. God says:

> Be ye not unequally yoked together with unbelievers: for what fellowship hath righteousness with unrighteousness? and what communion hath light with darkness? And what concord hath Christ with Belial? Or what part hath he that believeth with an infidel?
>
> And what agreement hath the temple of God with idols? for ye are the temple of the living God; as God hath said, I will dwell in them, and walk in them; and I will be their God, and they shall be my people.

By Bible standards, the leaders of many of America's large denominations and the pastors of their churches are unbelievers. Their words, the books they write or permit to be published, the Sunday School literature they distribute mark them as infidels.

God's Word commands the Christian not to be yoked together unequally with unbelievers. This does not mean that we should not welcome unsaved people into our church services or try to win them to Christ — but we should not enter into spiritual relationships with them. The Christian has Christ in his heart — and the unsaved man is still a child of the devil. The Scripture says, "What concord hath Christ with Belial (the devil)?" What spiritual food and light can the Christian get from a preacher who either doesn't know the Gospel — or doesn't preach it? What should you do? God doesn't leave room for argument or discussion. He concludes this passage, saying:

> Wherefore come out from among them, and be ye separate, saith the Lord, and touch not the unclean thing; and I will receive you, And will be a Father unto you, and ye shall be my sons and daughters saith the Lord Almighty.
> Having therefore these promises, dearly beloved, let us cleanse ourselves from all filthiness of the flesh and spirit, perfecting holiness in the fear of God. (II Corinthians 6:17-7:1)

Are you in a church which is part of the ecumenical movement and the National Council of Churches? Does your church fail to regularly and forcefully bring you face-to-face with *your* need of salvation and the new birth? If so, God says, "Come out from among them and be ye separate." Will you obey God?

Chapter VII

Nothing New Under the Sun

> *Thus saith the Lord. Stand by the roads and
> look, and ask for the eternal paths, where is the
> good, old way; then walk in it, and you will
> find rest for your souls.*
>
> — *Jeremiah 6:16*

IN EVERY GENERATION men believe that the problems they face are unique — that they are more threatened and closer to disaster than any other men who ever lived down through history. However, man doesn't change — and his problems change very little. The wisest man who ever lived, King Solomon, said:

> Is there anything whereof it may be said, See, this is
> new? It hath already been of old time, which was before
> us . . . and there is no new thing under the sun. (Ecclesiastes
> 1:9-10).

This is an age of revolution — but there have been revolutionary ages before. England — and all of Europe — were in turmoil in the late 17th and early 18th Centuries. Men were demanding political, economic, and spiritual freedom. As all the old ties with the past were broken, political and moral decay resulted. Of England during this period, a one-hundred year-old history records:

> Corruption and mismanagement in high places were the
> rule . . . Bribery among all classes was open, unblushing,
> and profuse . . . adultery, fornication, gambling, swearing,
> Sabbath Breaking and drunkeness were hardly regarded as
> vices at all. They were the fashionable practices of the
> people in the highest ranks of society . . . such was England
> in the 18th Century.[1]

Revolutionary societies and conspiratorial groups which were forerunners of communism placed their members in high places in the churches and in government.[2] Seats in Parliament were sold for $20,000. Distribution of pornographic literature was a serious problem. There was even a "God is dead" movement. A noted church historian looked at the decay and corruption, and said:

> Christianity seemed to lie as one dead, inasmuch that you might have said, "She is dead."[3]

The clergy, witnessing the collapse of morality, decency, and order in society and the seeming inability of the church to reach the masses with the age-old message, quit trying. They dropped what bare skeleton of the Christian doctrine remained in their formal services and liturgy and attempted to "restate Christianity in a formula which all could accept." By stripping Christianity of what was regarded as its "superstitious elements" they hoped to "make the natural rather than the supernatural the basis of belief." Compare these desperation efforts of an unregenerate clergy 250 years ago with the proposals of Bishop James Pike today. Pike says:

> Christianity is undergoing a rapid decline in England and Europe, and there are beginning signs of the same thing here in the United States. The situation is saddening . . . but worth observing. To me it underlines the urgency of saying what we mean in clear and relevant terms and abandoning categories that no longer have any meaning . . . The rejection of meaningless doctrines such as the Trinity, the Virgin Birth, and the Divinity of Jesus is necessary for the future health of the Christian Church.[4]

There is nothing new under the sun! The Deism movement which stripped 18th Century "Christianity" of its "superstitious and supernatural elements" also robbed it of its supernatural power to change men's hearts. Bishop Pike and like thinkers in major denominations have done the same thing to America's churches today.

A collection of letters by an 18th Century English preacher gives a concise account of the progressive deterioration which followed — and the force which ultimately halted the decay. The introduction of *Letters of John Newton* says . . .

> . . . England was in a state of religious and moral decay. For many years the land had been sinking into darkness and paganism. Intemperance and immorality, crime and cruelty were increasingly becoming the characteristics of the age.[5]

This could be a description of the crime, violence and moral decay in America today. The report continues.

The National Church was in such a dead condition that instead of being the salt, preserving the nation from corruption, she was only adding to the immorality by weakening the restraints which Christianity imposes on the lusts of men . . .

Today, the National Council of Churches "weakens the restraints" Christianity is supposed to impose on men by issuing booklets which tell young people "for the Christian there are no laws, no rules, no regulations . . ." Denominational leaders condone homosexuality "if both parties really love each other." Truly, there is nothing new under the sun!

WHAT SAVED ENGLAND?

After reviewing the seriousness of the situation, the report concluded:

If the nation was to be saved the Church would first have to be revived. And that is what took place. What the arm of the flesh could not do the arm of omnipotence accomplished. God was pleased to send a mighty revival which in the course of 50 years transformed the religious and moral life of the land.

Another commentator, J. C. Ryle, the Bishop of Liverpool, England a hundred years later, looked back on this period and wrote:

That a great change for the better came over England during the eighteenth century is a fact which I suppose no well-informed person would ever attempt to deny . . . But by what agency was this great change effected?[6]

Many today look to politics and politicians to solve the nation's problems, but Bishop Ryle said of the transformation of England in the 1700s:

The government of the country can lay no claim to the credit for the change. Morality cannot be called into being by penal enactments and statutes. People were never yet made religious by Acts of Parliament . . . Nor yet did the change come from the Church of England, as a body. The leaders of that venerable communion were utterly unequal to the times.[7]

The Bible-believing fundamentalists and religious separatists of the day were called "Dissenters." Even they had little effect, according to Bishop Ryle, who said:

Nor yet did the change come from the Dissenters. Content with their hardly-won triumphs, that worthy body of men seemed to rest upon their oars . . . (and) forgot the vital principles of their forefathers, and their own duties and responsibilities.

What, then, were the forces which held back the revolutionary tide in the 18th century? When all else had failed, God raised up a few men — John Wesley, George Whitefield and a handful of others. They were men who had both fundamentalist beliefs *and* a zeal to see men saved. They did His work in the old apostolic way, by becoming the evangelists of their day. Bishop Ryle said of them:

> They preached everywhere . . . in the pulpit of a church . . . a barn . . . in the field or in a market place . . . wherever hearers could be gathered, the spiritual reformers of the 18th century talked to men about their souls.
>
> They preached simply . . . the sufficiency and supremacy of Holy Scripture . . . the total corruption of human nature . . . that Christ's death upon the Cross was the only satisfaction for man's sin . . . that faith was the one thing men needed in order to obtain an interest in Christ's work for their souls.[9]

They taught that there was an inseparable connection between true faith and personal holiness. They taught that when a person really believed he became "a new creature in Christ" and that the change was manifested in every area of his life.

Wesley, Whitefield and the others were labelled "fanatics" and "extremists"[9] and barred from many churches. They were rejected by an unregenerate clergy because they taught the *universal necessity* of *heart* conversion and a new birth *even* for those who had been baptized as infants and confirmed into the church. Everywhere, they proclaimed to the crowds, "Ye must be born again" (John 3:7). The results were thrilling to behold. For example:

George Whitefield went to a coal mining town near Bristol in February 1739. Standing upon a hill, he began to preach to about 100 miners. As the working day in the coal pits ended, the number of hearers rapidly increased. Soon the congregation totaled many thousands of black-faced coal miners.

Whitefield preached of a God who loved sinful man so much that He sent His Son to suffer the punishment man deserved. He proclaimed the "good news" that all who believed could have forgiveness of sin and a new birth. Hundreds of hardened miners were convicted of their sin and rebellion against God and were supernaturally converted. The power of the message became evident, Whitefield recorded in his journal, when white streaks started appearing on the blackened cheeks of the miners. Their tears had washed the coal dust from their faces. Whitefield said:

> The change was evident to all, though numbers chose to impute it to anything rather than the finger of God.[10]

Soon the travelling evangelists had to move on to the next town. When they did, men and women on fire for the Saviour who had given them a new life started Bible classes and prayer groups. On their own, they started to preach judgment for sinners and the love of the Saviour to all who would listen.

They attacked decay and decadence in government, business and the church. Even though less than 2½% of the population was converted during Wesley's 50 year ministry, the face of England was changed.[11] As that handful became the "salt of the earth" the slave trade was stopped. Four out of five taverns were closed for lack of business. Prison and penal reforms were instituted. The dangerous conditions under which children worked in factories were improved — and corruption in government declined.

Professor Elie Halevy in his multi-volume *History of the English People* said the spiritual awakening provided the . . .

> . . . moral cement which restrained the plutocrats who had newly arisen from the masses from vulgar ostentation and debauchery, and placed over the proletariat a select body of workmen, enamoured of virtue and capable of self-restraint. Evangelicalism . . . restored in England the balance momentarily destroyed by the explosion of the revolutionary forces.[12]

The same revolutionary forces which ate at the heart of England in the early 18th century troubled France and most of the continent also. England turned to Jesus Christ and laid the foundations for the political freedom which Britain and America have enjoyed for 200 years. The French instead rebelled against the corrupt and decadent church — and against God as well. Their revolution degenerated into total rejection of the established economic, social and moral order. France has never recovered. Every generation of Frenchmen since has seen its land overrun by a foreign conqueror — or ruled by a domestic dictator. The revolution came later to Germany, Italy and Spain. Without reformation or a revival of true Bible Christianity, each has suffered similarly from almost continual political and economic turmoil.

The dramatically different way the revolutionary forces which troubled France and England developed demonstrate the truth of General Douglas MacArthur's words:

> History fails to record a single precedent in which nations subject to moral decay have not passed into political and economic decline. There has been either a spiritual awakening to overcome the moral lapse, or a progressive deterioration leading to ultimate national disaster.

In 1922, the British Prime Minister David Lloyd George stated that Great Britain . . .

> . . . owed more to the movement of which Wesley was the inspirer and leader, than to any other movement in the whole of its history . . . It civilized the people . . . There was a complete revolution effected in the whole country . . . it has given a different outlook to the British and American people from the outlook of the Continentals.[13]

Lord Baldwin, during his term as prime minister, said that historians . . .

> . . . who filled their pages with Napoleon and had nothing to say of John Wesley, now realize that they cannot explain nineteenth century England until they can explain Wesley. And I believe it is equally true to say, that you cannot understand twentieth century America, unless you understand Wesley.[14]

Even so, the Rev. Dr. Martin E. Marty, an official of the Lutheran Church Missouri Snyod and an associate editor of the ultra-liberal, ecumenical weekly magazine *Christian Century* has charged:

> In the industrial revolution of the eighteenth century, the church failed the world because it was not part of that revolution . . . The church managed to survive the 1700s while many institutions did not . . . but it was a dismal failure as a driving force in the revolution.[15]

Dr. Marty is correct that the Wesley revival was not

part of the revolution. It was the force which protected England and the United States from the horror, bloodshed, terror and tyranny which the revolution brought to France — and later to Germany, Italy, and Spain. This is the revolution many churchmen are actively promoting in America today.

THE REVIVAL IN AMERICA

As the words of David Lloyd George and Lord Baldwin indicated, the revival spread to America. The 30th President of the United States, Calvin Coolidge, said:

> America was born in a revival of religion. Back of that revival were John Wesley, George Whitefield, and Francis Asbury.[16]

In his autobiography, Ben Franklin provides an eyewitness account of how God worked during that revival to change men's hearts — and the whole face of America. When Whitefield came to America, 31-year old Ben Franklin was among the multitudes who thronged to hear him preach — in the churches and in the streets.

In his writings, Franklin expressed amazement at the "extraordinary influence" Whitefield's words had on the crowds "notwithstanding his common abuse of them that they were naturally beasts and devils."[17]

George Whitefield emphasized the "total depravity of man." His first goal was to show men that in God's sight all men are unclean and incapable of making themselves good enough for God — that their own good works are "as filthy rags in the sight of God." In the words of the Scriptures:

> . . . there is no difference: for all have sinned and come short of the glory of God . . . the wicked shall be turned into Hell . . . for the wages of sin is death . . . (Psalm 9:17, Romans 3:22-23, 6:23)

Men who came to see they had no righteousness of their own to offer God were ready to hear the good news of the Gospel. Whitefield then proclaimed the love of the God who sent His sinless Son to suffer and die as sinful man's substitute. He pleaded with sinners to invite the risen Son of God into their hearts to be their life. Whitefield frequently preached from the text in I Corinthians 1:30 which says:

> But of Him (God) are ye in Christ Jesus, who of God
> is made unto us wisdom, and righteousness; and santification,
> and redemption.

When God looks upon those who have asked Christ to
be their Saviour. He sees not their sins, but the righteousness of Jesus Christ. This was the simple and supernatural
message that transformed America 30 years before the
Revolutionary War. Whitefield preached this message in
Boston, New York, Philadelphia — and in towns large and
small all the way to Georgia. Men by the thousands faced
their sin and the punishment they deserved from God.
God's Holy Spirit supernaturally melted the hearts of
businessmen and church leaders, bartenders and drunkards.
When they fully realized how God loved them in spite of
their sin, they opened their hearts and became "new
creatures in Christ." Ben Franklin reported the results this
way:

> It was wonderful to see the change soon made in the
> manners of our inhabitants. From being thoughtless or
> indifferent about religion, it seemed as if all the world
> were growing religious, so that one could not walk thro'
> the town in an evening without hearing psalms sung in
> different families of every street.[18]

This was the atmosphere in which America was born.
The people — and their schools and churches and government — were changed. When George Whitefield preached
in Boston 22 preachers were converted. *Even Harvard
University was affected.* Before Whitefield came to Boston,
the president of Harvard University wrote to a friend
complaining of the moral decay in the college. He said:

> Whence is there such a prevalency of so many immorali-
> ties amongst the professors? Why so little success of the
> gospel?[19]

Later, describing the revival which came to the Harvard
campus, President Willard wrote:

> That which forbodes the most lasting advantage is the
> new state of the college. Gentlemen's sons that were sent
> here only for a mere polite education, are now so full of
> zeal for the cause of Christ and the love of souls as to
> devote themselves absolutely to the study of divinity. The
> college is entirely changed; the students are full of God —
> and will I hope come out blessings to this and succeeding
> generations.[20]

Some of our founding fathers were among the Harvard students who heard Whitefield preach in 1739. Others attended churches whose pulpits were filled by men converted under Whitefield's ministry — pulpits which were "aflame with righteousness."

America was born in this period of spiritual revival. It has been living since on the spiritual and political foundations laid by men who believed and obeyed God's command to . . .

> . . . render to Caesar the things that are Caesar's, and to God the things that are God's. (Mark 12:17)

Americans of this generation have made a mockery of the fulfillment of both responsibilities. As Alexis de Tocqueville, the French political philosopher who witnessed the fruits of the first revival, warned . . .

> . . . if America ever ceases to be good, America will cease to be great.

America has ceased to be good. Will she cease to be great? Will America turn back to God as England did under Wesley and Whitefield — or must she take the path of France whose revolution culminated . . .

> . . . in the Reign of Terror when Paris gutters ran red with human blood; when a prostitute was crowned Goddess of Reason: and when each new champion of freedom, crying "Liberty, Equality, and Fraternity," rushed his fellow champions to the guillotine, lest they rush him there first. So ended the first French Republic, denying all spiritual values and mocking God.[21]

Can America escape a similar fate? God warns:

> Like as ye have forsaken me, and served strange gods in your land, so shall ye serve strangers in a land that is not yours. (Jeremiah 5:19)

Chapter VIII

If Communism Takes Over

> *And it shall come to pass, when ye shall say,*
> *Wherefore doeth the Lord our God all these*
> *things unto us? and then thou shalt answer*
> *them, like as ye have forsaken me, and served*
> *strange gods in your land, so shall ye serve*
> *strangers in a land that is not yours.*
> — *Jeremiah 5:19*

IF AMERICA DOESN'T turn back to God, it must face the "progressive deterioration leading to national disaster" of which General MacArthur warned. If this happens, communism or some other form of tyranny will come to America. What will it mean for you and your family?

Congressional committees have provided an answer to that question by interviewing refugees from 20 countries the communists have conquered. Congress has documented and exposed the mass liquidation of millions of Chinese, Russians, Poles, Hungarians, Latvians, Cubans, etc. Planned starvation, the firing squad, and the slow agonizing death of the slave labor camp are among the execution methods the Reds have used.

Rev. Shih-ping Wang, East Asia director of the Baptist Evangelization Society, told the House Committee on Un-American Activities what happened to the individual when communism took China. Mr. Wang testified:

> The family unit is broken up. Husbands and wives are separated in different barracks. The children are taken away from the parents and placed in government-run nurseries. Husbands and wives meet only once a week for two hours— they have no other contact . . . The parents may see their children once a week and when they see them they can show no affection toward their children. Names are taken away from children and they are given numbers. There is no individual identity.[1]

In China, 40-million people were liquidated during the

first five years of communist rule. Mr. Wang told how some of them died:

> All the elderly people 60 years of age and above who cannot work are put in the old people's "Happy Home." After they are placed in the homes they are given shots. They are told these shots are for their health. But after the shots are taken they die within two weeks. After they die, the corpses are placed in vats. When the bodies decay and maggots set in, the maggots are used to feed the chickens. The remainder of the body is used for fertilizer.[2]

A young journalist, Kyung Rai Kim, now religious editor of a leading Seoul, Korea newspaper, told the congressional committees about persecution and murder of thousands of Christians when communism came to Korea. Mr. Kim said:

> An evangelist friend of mine, Lee Chang Whan, was killed . . . He was killed by the communists because he was trying to publish the Bible in secret . . . The Red police stripped him naked, bound him, and put him in an empty water pool. It was 17 degrees below zero that day. They filled the pool solid. My friend froze to death in 30 minutes. Then the police exhibited his body to the people.[3]

The communists do not simply execute enemies of the state. They practice planned, deliberate terror on the individual and then display the results to intimidate others. Mr. Kim continued:

> A lady evangelist, Kim Keum Sun, was tied between two horses. Then the horses were sent running in different directions. This happened in 1951 . . . She was guilty of not letting a portrait of the chief of Northern Korea be placed in her church.
>
> In January 1951, 250 pastors were killed by the Communists on the same day in the same place at Hong Jai Dong, Seoul, Korea. The Red police made holes through the pastors' hands with an ax and bound them with wire rope, and then they shot them. In February 1951, at Wong Dang church, Red soldiers burned 83 Christians to death with gasoline.[4]

Similar atrocities, designed to discourage man's worship of God, are reported wherever communism has come to power. Dr. Thomas Dooley, the young American doctor who gave his life while establishing hospitals to help the people of Vietnam, wrote three books. They include detailed descriptions of atrocities carried out by the Viet Cong against the people they say they are trying to help. One such incident shows what happens when communists gain control in an area. Dr. Dooley wrote:

> Having set up their controls in the village of Haiduoung, Communists visited the village schoolhouse and took seven children out of class and into the courtyard. All were ordered to sit on the ground, and their hands were tied behind their backs. Then they brought out one of the young teachers, with hands also tied. Now the new classes began.[5]

The children were charged with treason. An informer had reported to police that these children had been attending secret classes conducted by their teacher at night. The subject of the classes was *religion*. As a punishment, the seven children were to be deprived of their hearing. Dr. Dooley described how it was done:

> Two Viet Minh (communist) guards went to each child and one of them firmly grasped the head between his hands. The other then rammed a wooden chopstick into each ear. He jammed it in with full force. The stick split the ear canal wide open and tore the ear drum. The shrieking of the children was heard all over the village.
>
> Both ears were stabbed in this fashion. The children screamed and wrestled and suffered horribly. Since their hands were tied behind them, they could not pull the wood out of their ears. They shook their heads and squirmed about, trying to make the sticks fall out. Finally they were able to dislodge them by scraping their heads against the ground.[6]

To prevent the teacher from teaching again — and as a warning to others against teaching children about Jesus Christ — the communist guards pulled the teacher's tongue out with a pair of pliers and cut it off. He was left to drown in his own blood. These victims were brought to Dr. Dooley's hospital from the communist-controlled areas for treatment. Recounting dozens of such incidents, he wrote:

> The purpose of this book is not to sicken anyone or to dwell upon the horror . . . But I do want to show what has come upon these people of the Delta. And justice demands that some of the atrocities we learned of in Haiphong be put on record . . .
>
> Early in my Haiphong stay I was puzzled not only by the growing number but by the character of Communist atrocities. So many seemed to have religious significance.

More and more, I was learning that these punishments were linked to man's belief in God.[7]

This is not the picture of communism which the TV networks presented when they dramatized Dr. Dooley's life and work. This is not the picture of communism President Eisenhower helped to present to the world when he had his grandson photographed on the butcher Khrushchev's knee. This is not the picture of communism the Kremlin presents to the world when Kosygin joins President Johnson on nationwide TV to announce that they are both interested in peace for their grandchildren. This is communism in action. It is the fulfillment of the words of Lenin who said:

> We have never rejected terror on principle, nor can we do so. Terror is a form of military operation that may be usefully applied.[8]

Dr. Dooley died in 1961. The communist reign of terror in Vietnam continues as he described it. Single paragraphs from three different newspaper stories published in 1967 show continued communist disregard for human life and their use of terror as a weapon of oppression. The stories read:

> In the worst civilian massacre of the war, the Viet Cong killed at least 121 tribespeople, most of them women and children, in apparent reprisal for a village's refusal to supply recruits for the guerillas.[9]

The communists frequently ignore military targets to massacre civilians as this story shows:

> In the night attack on Dai Loc, the Communists passed up an easy chance to destroy a key military bridge or to overrun the government's district headquarters. Instead they pressed their attack against the refugees . . . because a large number of them had come out of areas long under communist control.[10]

When American bombs accidentally kill civilians, headlines tell the story. This Viet Cong atrocity was reported far down in a routine war story:

> From the Mekong Delta 40 miles south of Saigon came word of the killing of 10 Vietnamese children and the wounding of 16 more when they were used as human shields by Viet Cong advancing against a unit of South Vietnamese rangers.[11]

This is not the image of the Viet Cong that Dr. Benjamin

Spock, Martin Luther King, Bobby Kennedy, and the National Council of Churches present to the world. When they denounce America's efforts to keep communists from taking control of all Vietnam, they portray the Viet Cong as a popularly-supported nationalist movement interested only in getting freedom for their people. If Kennedy, King, and Spock are correct and the VC do have the support of the people, why must they resort to such terror tactics?

This terror does not cease even when communism is firmly established. Dr. Jurgen Dennert, a correspondent for a German news magazine, was in Peiping in 1966 when the Red Guards were unleashed on the people. His shocked eye-witness account was reported in America by the liberal editor and columnist Ralph McGill who quoted Dennert as saying:

> I have never seen such brutality and cruelty. The attacks seemed directed mostly at older persons . . . I saw several persons beaten to death and others so savagely treated by the flailing of heavy sticks of steel or wood that many of them must have surely died.
>
> One of the sights I shall never forget was the treatment of two old persons. Their belongings had been brought from their rooms and piled on the street and set afire. The guards then took the old man and woman by the neck and thrust their bodies into the smoke and so near the flames they were seared. There were many instances of old couples having their belongings pulled out of their rooms and destroyed. The two tortured by fire were more unlucky.[12]

This wave of terror swept China in 1966 and 1967, seventeen years after communism came to China.

IN RUSSIA TODAY

In the 50 years since the revolution, the Soviet Union has supposedly "mellowed." Vocal opponents of communism were long ago liquidated. Those who have survived have learned how to live within the framework of a police state. Even so, the state continues its program of organized, planned terror. In August 1966, for example, Associated Press reported from Moscow:

> Six members of a Baptist sect have been sentenced to prison terms of unspecified length on charges of anti-social activities and influencing children's minds with books containing "non-sensical ideas on reality."

The newspaper *Uchitelskaya Gazetta* said . . . the sect leaders set up an illegal Sunday School in which illiterate and fanatical teachers taught "God's word" to children 8 to 11 years old.[13]

Over 250 such trials were held in many parts of the Soviet Union in 1966.[14] They are a part of the worldwide communist campaign of terror to discourage belief in the true and living God which Dr. Dooley observed. The "Reverend" Alexander Karev, general secretary of the government-sanctioned Baptist Union in the USSR, approved of the jail sentences for the Christian leaders. He said that the groups operating the Sunday Schools were "small and fanatical sects" which were not approved by the regular Baptists.[15] Karev and other representatives of state-controlled "churches" participate in meetings with the National and World Councils of Churches and the Baptist World Alliance. They have been paraded across America by liberal churchmen as "proof" that there is religious freedom in the Soviet Union.

Terror is used in Vietnam to discourage those who would flee from the communists. Terror is used the same way in Europe. From 1949 until the Berlin Wall was erected 2,824,000 East Germans fled from the workers "paradise." Since the Wall was built in 1961, only 25,500 persons have escaped. During the first six months of 1967, only 500 people came through or over the Wall compared with 1736 the year before, 2329 in 1965, and 3155 in 1964. The number declined each year because terror takes its toll. Communist guards shot and killed 133 persons trying to escape during the Wall's first six years.[16] Communism has not changed — in the Soviet Union or Vietnam! As Lenin said:

We have never rejected terror on principle, nor can we do so.

Why do most Americans ignore the words of Lenin, the testimony of Dr. Dooley, the warnings of J. Edgar Hoover and others? Why, in the face of all the evidence to the contrary, do most Americans choose to believe that communism is "changing" and "mellowing?" The Scriptures prophecy that in the last days men will believe what they want to believe. In II Timothy 4:3-4, the Apostle Paul wrote:

For the time will come when they will not endure sound doctrine (teaching); but after their own lusts shall they heap to themselves teachers, having itching ears; And they shall turn away their ears from the truth, and shall be turned unto fables.

Some of the language in these verses is outdated and hard to understand. The truth they teach, however, is still applicable. Paul was telling young Timothy that men have a tendency to reject the truth if it is unpleasant. They will seek, instead, teachers and leaders who will tell them what they want to hear. Why is this true?

There are many reasons why man won't face his problems. Man, by nature, doesn't like to face unpleasantness. Every day people die because they hoped that the lump, the pain, or the growing mole which warned of cancer would go away. When they finally faced the truth *it was too late*. Men, similarly, won't face the threat of communism, hoping that it will go away. Others get so busy fulfilling business, family and social obligations that they never take time to look at the world around them. They use their "busy-ness" as an excuse for refusing to even look at the problem.

Many who suspect that communism does pose a real threat also refuse to investigate the threat. They know if the problem is real they will have to do something about it. They will have to alert others to the danger. They will have to work politically to replace blind leaders in Washington. They know that if the threat of communism is real, they will have to devote their lives to keeping America free.

Those who take such a stand are ridiculed. They are labelled extremists. They become unpopular. They often have to leave their church. Sometimes their business suffers. Rather than risk these consequences, it is easier, for a time, for men to believe the TV networks, the news magazines, the editorial columnists, and the political leaders who teach the fable that communism is "mellowing." As the Apostle Paul said, men . . .

. . . shall turn away their ears from the truth, and shall be turned unto fables.

They need to face the question the Lord Jesus asked when He said:

For what is a man profited, if he shall gain the whole world, and lose his own soul? Or what shall a man give in exchange for his soul? (Matthew 16:26)

Men who refuse to face the threat of communism may someday find that they have exchanged their freedom for temporary peace of mind, the approval of men or the time to accumulate more of the world's goods. They will lose all of these things if the communists take over.

Many people who have faced the threat of communism and are doing something about it, are ignoring an even greater threat — for many of the same reasons. They ignore the certainty of Hell which is ahead for all who die without being saved.

As awful as communism is, its torments last just for an instant — or perhaps for a lifetime. The tortures of Hell are without end. The Lord Jesus warned of the danger in facing earthly perils such as communism and ignoring eternity. He said:

> And fear not them which kill the body, but are not able to kill the soul; but rather fear him which is able to destroy both soul and body in hell. (Matthew 10:28)

A communist takeover of America is only a possibility (becoming more probable the longer the threat is ignored). Hell is a certainty for all who die without having been born again by accepting Jesus Christ as personal Saviour.

Rather than face this danger, men instead turn to the myths and fables of those who ridicule, ignore or deny the reality of Hell and punishment for sin.

It was of this departure from spiritual truths that Paul was actually writing when he said that the time would come when men would turn away from the truth and find teachers who would teach them what they want to hear. Because of loyalty to church, family or friends, an unwillingness to think about death and judgment, or perhaps a desire to cling to sin, men refuse to come to Christ for a new birth. They are exchanging their souls for whatever keeps them from accepting God's gift of salvation.

Chapter IX

Can America be Saved?

Wherefore thus saith the Lord God of Hosts,
Because ye speak this word, behold, I will
make my words in thy mouth fire, and this
people wood, and it shall devour them.
— Jeremiah 5:14

MAN HAS TO see himself as a sinner before he can be saved. So also does America need to be brought face-to-face with the treachery and wickedness in the White House, the Court, the Congress and the Church.

America needs to see herself — and then hear this warning which God gave Israel 2600 years ago.

Shall I not visit for these things? saith the Lord: shall not my soul be avenged on such a nation as this? (Jeremiah 5:29)

Exposing evil and warning the wicked in a land which has turned its back on God and His Word may look like an impossible task. Fortunately, however, revivals — and salvation by faith in Jesus Christ — do not have to start with an intellectual acceptance of the Bible as God's Word. The Word of God is the starting point. When preached, it builds its own foundation in a supernatural way.

John Wesley didn't defend the Bible. He preached it — and God used the Word to turn England upside down. When George Whitefield preached to the congregation of hardened coal miners 230 years ago at Kingwood in England,[1] he didn't start his message with a theological dissertation on the proofs for the Bible. Instead, he simply preached the Word of God, which is . . .

. . . quick and powerful, and sharper than any two-edged sword, piercing even to the dividing asunder of soul and marrow and is a discerner of the thoughts and intents of the heart. (Hebrews 4:12)

The word of God strips away man's pretensions and the

things he'd like to believe about himself and shows him his own heart. Whitefield used the Bible to tell men that they were sinners. They saw themselves in the Word which he preached because the Word of God is like *a looking glass*. (James 1:23-25)

Through the Word, the men heard of the penalty for sin and were warned. (Psalm 19:11) As they heard of the Saviour who died to pay the penalty they deserved, the Word *melted* (Psalm 147:18) their hardened hearts. Through the preaching of the Word, God gave them the *faith* to believe . . .

> . . . for faith cometh by hearing, and hearing by the Word of God. (Romans 10:17)

The Word of God, when preached, builds faith in itself. It is its own foundation. It has a supernatural effect on the ears and the heart of those who hear it. God *promises* that when His Word is sent forth . . .

> . . . it shall not return unto me void, but it shall accomplish that which I please, and it shall prosper in the thing whereto I sent it. (Isaiah 55:11)

WHAT CAN WE DO?

Exposing America's wickedness and proclaiming judgment to come from God's Word — for the individual and the nation — is the challenge. Born-again Christians should be doing this job. Too many of them, however, are like the fundamentalists in John Wesley's day. They pay lip service to their responsibilities to take God's Word to those around them. However, in their hearts they say, "That's why we hired the preacher."

America will be turned back to God — and political sanity — when Christians again come to an understanding *and acceptance* of why God gives ministers to the church. The Scriptures teach that God . . .

> . . . gave some (churches), apostles; and some, prophets; and some, evangelists; and some, pastors and teachers; *for the perfecting of the saints for the work of the ministry* . . . (Ephesians 4:11-12)

Pastors are charged with teaching the born-again believers (saints) how to witness for Christ and win people to Him. They should learn in church how to start and teach neighborhood Bible classes and lead prayer groups. When Christians again fulfill these Biblical responsibilities (as the new born "babes" did in Wesley's day and the new Christians did in the first century) revival will result and the nation will be changed.

In 1964, over 1.5-million concerned Americans involved themselves in the presidential campaign of Senator Barry Goldwater. They gave money, signed petitions, wrote and distributed books, and rang doorbells.

In one area of north St. Louis county, in Missouri, over 300 persons worked door-to-door from May to November visiting every house in an area with 100,000 people. As many as five return visits were made with literature, books, etc. to any house where there was a chance to change a vote. These door-to-door canvassers told those they visited that . . .

> Political parties change their beliefs. The party your grandfather voted for no longer exists. This is an important election. Examine your beliefs and what the candidates believe. Support and vote for the man who will best represent you.

On November 7, 1964, as a result of this effort and a small population increase, Barry Goldwater got 14,000 votes in an area where Richard Nixon had the support of 12,000 people four years before. It didn't bring victory, however, because America's problem is not basically political — it is a moral problem.

Recognizing this fact, what would happen if a group of spirit filled Christians would go door-to-door with the message . . .

> . . . Churches have been changing a lot of their basic beliefs. There is a good possibility that the church your grandfather belonged to no longer preaches the Bible messages he heard as a boy. Have you checked your own beliefs against the Bible? Jesus taught, "Except a man be born again, he shall not see the kingdom of God." Have you been born again?

Those who indicated a positive interest or need would be visited again and again. Living room Bible study classes could be organized for those wanting to know more about the Word of God. At a time when churches are changing creeds and convictions many people want to know what the Bible says. However, they need someone "to guide them" (Acts 8:26-39).

The results of such a campaign would be felt — not just in one election — but for 50 years to come. The spiritual and moral climate of the area would be changed. Its politics would become more conservative also.

Such efforts could stimulate the revival which can save America.

Will Christians do this job? Will they work as hard for Jesus Christ as political conservatives and many Christians did for Barry Goldwater in 1964? There are unspeakable joys in telling lost sinners about Jesus — yet too many Christians today are like the Jews of Jeremiah's time. God told them . . .

> . . . your iniquities have turned these blessings away, and your sins have kept the good harvests from you . . . this people has a heart that draws back from God and a will that rebels against Him; they have revolted and quit His service. (Jeremiah 5:23, 25 — Amplified Bible)

The revival which can save America hasn't come because churches and Christians have lost all concept of the real nature of sin. Many born-again Christians who never miss church and don't smoke, drink, dance, or go to movies are still living in deep sin. Christians who wouldn't think of disobeying God's commandments against lying, adultery, Sabbath-breaking, murder, etc. regularly ignore one or more of the positive commands to . . .

> . . . study His Word (I Timothy 2:15) . . . witness and preach the gospel to everyone we meet (Acts 1:8, Psalm 107:2) . . . pray without ceasing (I Thessalonians 5:17) . . . come out of unbelieving churches (II Corinthians 6:14-17) . . . feed on His Word daily (Matthew 4:4) . . . become like Jesus Christ (Romans 8:29, 12:2) . . . and render to Caesar (Luke 20:25)

Can America be saved? God promises *He* will save us and heal our land — if we meet His conditions. *God has promised*:

> If my people, which are called by my name, shall humble themselves, and pray, and seek my face, and turn from their wicked ways; then will I hear from heaven, and will forgive their sin, and will heal their land (II Chronicles 7:14).

This is a *promise* to God's children. If born-again Christians will turn from their wicked ways (failing to pray, witness, study the Word, be the salt of the earth, etc.) God *promises* that He will heal our land.

God kept this promise when He sent a revival to heal England in the 18th Century. He fulfilled these promises again in America just before the Civil War. In 1857, America was troubled much as the land is today. One commentator records:

> In the middle of the nineteenth century, religious life in America was in a decline . . . Political strife provoked tremendous interest . . . the slavery question was of paramount importance, and men's passions and energies were being diverted into the channels of contention on either side of the controversy.
>
> The zeal of the people was devoted to the accumulation of wealth. Other things, including religion, took a lesser place. Boom times — a wave of prosperity . . . caught the public fancy, and turned men's hearts away from God.[2]

Burdened by the conditions of the day, a quiet, zealous Christian businessman named Jeremiah Lanphier decided to invite others to join him in a noonday prayer meeting. Lanphier planned to meet once a week in New York's downtown business section to ask God to send a revival.[3] In response to handbills he distributed, six people showed up at noon the first Wednesday. Twenty attended the second week. On the third Wednesday, 40 men came to pray. A month after the prayer meetings started, the financial boom collapsed. Factories closed down and vast numbers were thrown out of work.

In the midst of all the trouble, Lanphier's prayer group continued to meet — *and grow*. Within six months, 10,000 businessmen were meeting at noon *daily* in New York City for prayer! They found out that the man who really prays for revival will soon feel it in his own heart — and see it spread as he gives out the Word of God to those he contacts. This is what happened in early 1858. Revival broke out and the prayer meetings — and the revival — spread to major cities all over America.

Within two years, a million souls had been saved and added to the membership of America's churches.[4] The revival spread around the world in five years as other millions were saved. Its effects were still being felt 50 years later at the start of World War I through the work and ministry of such great Christian leaders as D. L. Moody, J. Hudson Taylor, and the founder of the Salvation Army, William Booth.[5] All of these men started their lives of service for Christ during the Great Awakening.

That God answers prayer was uniquely demonstrated during the Awakening of 1858. The other distinctive characteristic of this revival was the role of the layman. A church historian of the period records:

> The revival of 1858 inaugurated in some sense the era of lay work in American Christianity . . . No new doctrine was brought forward, but *a new agency* was brought to bear in spreading the old truth through the efforts of men who, if they could not interpret the Scriptures with precision or train souls to perfection, could at least help inquiring sinners to find the Lord by relating how they themselves had found Him.
>
> Since Christianity is a religion of experience, this lay element was a power in the 1st Century church . . . but it dropped out of the Church when Christianity, ceasing to be an experience, was practiced only as a pompous system of priest-craft or taught as an abtuse philosophy of religion. It now returned in the regeneration of a nation.[6]

Another commentator relates similar comments regarding the role of the laymen in this great revival, saying . . .

> This divine visitation, providential in its character, was emphatically a lay revival . . . The revival was carried on independently of the ministry and almost without their aid. The ministry was not ignored, nor was there in any sense an opposition to them. They carried on their regular services, but to greatly increased congregations, which were the immediate fruits of the revival, and by their preaching and their prayers they gave encouragement to the work and cooperated with it . . .
>
> The movement commenced with a layman, it enlisted the sympathies of other laymen throughout the country, and it was carried on chiefly through their instrumentality . . . The revival, moreover served as a great training school for laymen and brought to light the abilities of such men as D. L. Moody, who has left a lasting impress upon the history of American Christianity.[7]

The Awakening of 1858 demonstrated the fruits of following the Bible way to revival. The Bible says God gives the churches ". . . pastors and teachers for the perfecting of the saints for the work of the ministry."

Can America be saved? What can you do? The Bible says:

> Let the high praises of God be in their mouth, and a two-edged sword in their hand (Psalm 149:6)

We are commanded to (1) praise God for what He has done for us. Then (2) we are to use the "two-edged sword" which is the Word of God to tell others how He will do the same thing for them. If we are saved, we are to tell others. God commands:

> Let the redeemed of the Lord say so. (Psalm 107:2)

When we tell others of the change the Lord has wrought in our lives he uses this testimony to demonstrate to the unsaved the truth and power of His Word. The Psalmist David described his salvation this way:

> I waited patiently for the Lord; and he inclined unto me and heard my cry. He brought me up also out of the miry clay and set my feet upon a rock and established my goings.
> And he hath put a new song in my mouth, even praise unto our God: many shall see it, and fear, and shall trust in the Lord. (Psalm 40:1-3)

Can you look back to a day when you cried out to the Lord for salvation? Do you remember how He lifted *you* out of the depths of sin and "put a new song" in your heart? If not, perhaps you are like John Wesley was. Wesley was a preacher's son who had been baptized, raised in a Christian home and trained in a seminary. He had preached for 12 years, but *he had never been born again.*

During his time as a missionary in America, Wesley became discouraged because nothing happened in the lives of men when he preached. As a result of the preaching of some Moravian missionaries Wesley saw drunks become sober citizens and wife beaters become model husbands and fathers. After his return to England, he slowly came to realize that his own heart had never been changed. Then one day, while listening to a reading from Martin Luther's commentary on the Epistle to the Romans, God saved John Wesley. He showed Wesley that salvation and a right relationship with Himself comes, not through our works and self effort to be holy, but as a gift. Salvation is a gift from God. God loved us so much that He put our sins on Jesus Christ so that He might apply the righteousness of Jesus to those who will believe. The Scriptures say:

> For if Abraham were justified by works, he hath whereof to glory; but not before God. For what saith the scripture? Abraham believed God, and it was counted to him for righteousness.
>
> Now to him that worketh is the reward not reckoned of grace, but of debt. But to him that worketh not, but believeth on him that justifieth the ungodly, his faith is counted for righteousness.
>
> Now it was not written for his sake alone, that it was imputed to him; but for us also, to whom it shall be imputed, if we believe on him that raised up Jesus our Lord from the dead: Who was delivered for [on account of] our offenses, and was raised again for [on account of] our justification. (Romans 4:2-5, 23-25)

John Wesley believed and became "a new creature in Christ." He set out across England preaching the message:

> Ye must be born again. (John 3:7)

John Wesley had been trying to get good enough through his own efforts to earn God's pleasure. He was like many today who hope they will get to Heaven because they do good works, belong to the "right" church, participate in certain religious services, do penance, practice self-denial and prayer. However, the Word of God says:

> For by grace are ye saved through faith; and that not of yourself: it is the gift of God: not of works lest any man should boast. (Ephesians 2:8-9)

We can't ever do enough works to deserve salvation. We are saved by faith in Jesus Christ. Once we are truly saved and know it, however, our salvation will show in our works. The Apostle James said:

> I will show thee my faith by my works. (James 2:18)

God sees the heart and looks only for your faith. Man looks upon your works.

If you have never been born again — and have come to see that you cannot save yourself — will you, right now, take the *gift* of salvation by asking Jesus Christ to come into your heart to be *your* Saviour? To all who will come to Him this way, He *promises*:

> . . . him that cometh to me I will in no wise cast out . . .
> for whosoever shall call upon the name of the Lord shall
> be saved. (John 6:37, Romans 10:13)

Once you have trusted Christ as Saviour, He should begin
to show in your life. Others should see that you are different
— that you have been raised from spiritual deadness and
given a new birth and new life. This truth is pictured in a
glorious way in the 12th Chapter of the Gospel of John.
After Jesus raised Lazarus from the dead (a picture of what
happens spiritually when a person gets saved), the Lord
was a guest at his home. The Scripture tells how crowds of
people came to see Jesus . . .

> . . . and they came not for Jesus sake only, but that they
> might see Lazarus also whom he had raised from the dead.
> But the chief priests consulted that they might put Lazarus
> also to death; because that *by reason of him many of the
> Jews went away, and believed on Jesus. (John 12:9-11)*

Jesus demonstrates his supernatural power today by rais-
ing men from spiritual deadness and making them "new
creatures in Christ." When others see the change in the lives
of born-again Christians, they "go-away and believe on
Jesus."

This is how revivals start. Do people see Jesus Christ in
you? Many American conservatives need to face this question
just as a patriot of another day faced it. Patrick Henry,
hearing that some people questioned whether he was a
Christian, said:

> I hear it is said . . . that some good people think I am
> no Christian. This thought gives me much more pain than
> the appellation of Tory; because I think religion is of
> infinitely higher importance than politics; and I find much
> cause to reproach myself, that I have lived so long, and
> have given no decided and public proofs of my being
> a Christian.[8]

If you have trusted Christ and *know* He is your Saviour,
let Him show His life through yours. Let Him use you to
start the revival which can save America. Use God's Word
to warn the wicked. Trust in the Lord God of Hosts who
said:

> Because ye speak this word, behold, I will make my
> words in thy mouth fire, and this people wood, and it
> shall devour them. (Jeremiah 5:14)

Will it work? God has regularly sent His servants to call rebellious and sinful people back to Him — with varying results.

About 750 years before Christ, the prophet Isaiah was sent to the children of Israel with the message . . .

> Come now, and let us reason together, saith the Lord: though your sins be as scarlet, they shall be as white as snow; though they be red like crimson, they shall be as wool.
> If ye be willing and obedient, ye shall eat the good of the land: But if ye refuse and rebel, ye shall be devoured with the sword: for the mouth of the Lord hath spoken it. (Isaiah 1:19-20)

When the Jews didn't listen, God sent Jeremiah to plead:

> Thus saith the Lord, stand ye in the old ways, and see, and ask for the old paths, where is the good way, and walk therein, and ye shall find rest for your souls. But they said, we will not walk therein. (Jeremiah 6:16)

Because Israel refused to heed God's repeated calls to return to Him, He sent them into captivity, saying:

> Like as ye have forsaken me, and served strange gods in your land, so shall ye serve strangers in the land that is not yours. (Jeremiah 5:19)

God's Word records many accounts of His judgment and chastisement falling on man and his world. When the earth was still young man became so corrupt and wicked God said:

> My spirit shall not always strive with man, for that he also is flesh: yet his days shall be an hundred and twenty years. (Genesis 6:3)

God called Noah and told him:

> The end of all flesh is come before me; for the earth is filled with violence through them; and, behold, I will destroy them with the earth. (Genesis 6:13)

Noah, a preacher of righteousness, labored for 120 years. Only seven people heeded the call to repent. Only seven persons believed God's message. They accepted His provision for their salvation. They were saved when the waters of judgment came because they had believed God.

Not all of the Bible accounts of God's dealing with man have such grim endings. Once, God called a man named Jonah to . . .

> . . . Arise, go to Nineveh, that great city, and cry against it; for their wickedness is come up before me. (Jonah 1:3)

Jonah was as rebellious as most Christians are today. When God ordered him to give out the word of warning, Jonah ran away. After God chastened Jonah three days and nights in the belly of the great fish, Jonah submitted. The Word of the Lord then came unto him a second time, saying:

> . . . Arise, go unto Nineveh, that great city, and preach unto it the preaching that I bid thee. (Jonah 3:2)

This time, Jonah obeyed God. He went to Nineveh and preached the message:

> Yet forty days, and Nineveh shall be overthrown. (Jonah 3:4)

The Bible only records that Jonah preached one sermon in this great city of 1½-million people, but . . .

> . . . the people of Nineveh believed God. (Jonah 3:5)

The people who heard Jonah repented, and started to repeat God's warning to others. Soon the King heard. He turned to God and sent a message to the whole city saying . . .

> . . . cry mightily unto God: yea, let them turn everyone from his evil way, and from the violence that is in their hands. Who can tell if God will turn and repent, and turn away from his fierce anger, that we perish not? (Jonah 3:8-9)

That's what happened. The people of Nineveh heeded the call to repent — and the Scriptures say:

> And God saw their works, that they turned from their evil way; and God repented: of the evil, that he had said he would do unto them; and he did it not. (Jonah 3:10)

Revivals start when people hear God's message of judgment, repent of their sins, and start giving out the warning to others.

What's ahead for America? We can't know. We are simply to obey God's command to warn the wicked. Christians have the same commission He gave to Ezekiel when He said:

> Son of man, I have made thee a watchman unto the house of Israel: therefore hear the word at my mouth and give them warning from me. (Ezekiel 3:17)

God may use the words of warning you give out for Him to start the revival which can save America. He may use them to save a remnant which will be His faithful underground church during a period of captivity. It may also be, that as in Noah's time, the earth is nearing the end of another age. The words of warning may be used to deliver just a handful from the wrath to come. Many believe that the world is entering into a final period of turmoil, trouble and apostasy. Such a time is prophesied to precede the personal return of Jesus Christ to put down wickedness and institute His reign over the earth.

America today must look forward to either revival, revolution — or the return of the Lord.

Chapter X

Are We Nearing the End of the Age?

Shall I not visit for these things? saith the Lord: shall not my soul be avenged on such a nation as this? —Jeremiah 5:29

BEFORE JESUS CHRIST ASCENDED into heaven, He promised His disciples "I will come again, and receive you unto myself." Of His ascension we read:

And while they looked stedfastly toward heaven as he went up, behold, two men stood by them in white apparel; Which also said, Ye men of Galilee, why stand ye gazing up into heaven? this same Jesus, which is taken up from you into heaven, shall so come in like manner as ye have seen him go into heaven. (Acts 1:10-11)

There are more than 300 Old and New Testament Scriptures which promise that Jesus will return to earth. He's coming to judge the wicked, put down evil, and to reign over His people for 1000 years. These promises are to be fulfilled just as literally as the 200 Old Testament prophecies of His virgin birth, death, burial and resurrection were fulfilled in His first coming when He suffered and died for man's sins.

Of His second coming, the Scriptures say:

Our God shall come, and shall not keep silence: a fire shall devour before him, and it shall be very tempestuous round about him. He shall call to the heavens from above, and to the earth, that he may judge his people. (Psalm 50:3-4)

Behold, he cometh with clouds; and every eye shall see him, and they also which pierced him: and all kindreds of the earth shall wail because of him. (Revelation 1:7)

Men scoff at this teaching — but even their ridicule and unbelief is one of the signs that the end of the age is drawing near. Of the prophecies of His coming, the Apostle Peter wrote:

> Knowing this first, that there shall come in the last days scoffers walking after their own lusts,
>
> And saying, Where is the promise of his coming? for since the fathers fell asleep, all things continue as they were from the beginning of creation . . . But the day of the Lord will come as a thief in the night. (II Peter 3:3-4, 10)

Informed conservatives and anti-communists who are also competent Bible scholars believe that these prophecies may be nearing fulfillment. They see the growth of world communism, the return of the Jews to Israel, and the coming one-world government and the one-world ecumenical church as phenomena which are prophesied to immediately precede the return of the Lord. They believe world events may herald His coming with His saints to fight the battle of Armageddon, defeat the devil, and institute His personal reign for 1000 years of peace during which "the lion will lay down with the lamb."

Bible prophecy concerning the possible end of this age stimulates many questions among churchgoers — and also among those who normally have only a passing interest in spiritual things. They ask:

> What has to happen yet on God's prophesied program before Jesus returns to straighten out the world's mess and institute His reign?
>
> What are the signs of His coming? Can we know anything about when? How do disarmament, world socialism, the United Nations and the ecumenical movement fit into prophecy?
>
> What will His coming mean to the Christian? What will happen to the Jew? What about the unsaved person? What will it mean to me?
>
> If the end of the age is near do we have any responsibility other than getting right with God and watching for His return?
>
> If all these things are prophesied and we oppose world government and the one-world church aren't we really opposing God's plan for the age?

WHAT IS GOD'S SCHEDULE?

Before the Lord Jesus Christ returns to earth to institute His reign and set all things right, the Scriptures prophecy . . .

. . . there shall be a time of trouble, such as never was since there was a nation even to that same time (Daniel 12:1).

This great and terrible time of tribulation will come when the Anti-Christ comes . . .

. . . even him, whose coming is after the working of Satan with all power and signs and lying wonders. (II Thessalonians 2:9)

The Anti-Christ will achieve complete political and economic control of the world. He will establish, in effect, a one-world socialist dictatorship. The Scriptures say . . .

. . . and power was given him over all kindreds and tongues and nations . . . and he causeth all, both small and great, rich and poor, free and bond, to receive a mark in their right hand, or in their foreheads: and that no man might buy or sell, save he had that mark, or the name of the beast, or the number of his name. (Revelation 13:7, 16,17)

The same picture of the Anti-Christ is found in the Old Testament as well. The prophet Daniel foresaw a one-world super government which would be separate from all other governments and kings and yet would rule over them (such as a strengthened United Nations might rule over all nations). In a vision, Daniel saw this last great kingdom . . .

. . . which shall be diverse from all kingdoms, and shall devour the whole earth, and shall tread it down and break it in pieces. (Daniel 7:23)

The Anti-Christ who will head this prophesied one-world system will be "a king of fierce countenance, skilled in intrigues, and his power shall be mighty." He will come to power as the world becomes more and more rotten morally. He will actually rise at a time of great crisis through treaties and covenants made to insure peace. "He shall come in peaceably," the Scriptures say, "and by peace he shall destroy many." Once he gets power "he shall work deceitfully" with a small but powerful force (like a greatly strengthened UN peace force) for a worldwide redistribution of the wealth. "He shall have power over the treasures of gold and silver, and over all precious things." (Daniel 8:23-25, 11:21-24, 43; Revelation 6:8)

Consider these 2500 year old prophecies in light of 1967 proposals for a world monetary system as the solution for the gold crisis[1] and a world banker who would control "all gold and silver." Consider these prophecies in light of proposals made by UN Secretary General U Thant for world-wide redistribution of the wealth through a United Nations graduated income tax.

Consider the prophecies *and the above proposals* in view of the "disarmament" plans in U.S. State Department Document 7277. This plan envisions all of the nations of the world transferring their weapons to the United Nations until . . .

> . . . no state would have the military power to challenge the progressively strengthened U.N. Peace Force.[2]

If carried out, this proposal would fulfill the Scriptural prophecy which says that the nations of the world will . . .

> . . . have one mind, and shall *give* their power and strength unto the beast. (Revelation 17:13)

After which, in the words of one very good modern paraphrase of Daniel 11:24 . . .

> He will enter the richest areas of the land without warning and do something never done before: he will take the property and wealth of the rich and scatter it out among the people.

Consider what would happen if American weapons are in the hands of a super government's peace force. There could be no resistance if the U.N. General Assembly (where America has only one vote) or a similar super-government body, decided to impose a world-wide graduated income tax (the bulk of which would be paid by Americans).

The propaganda campaign to influence Americans to turn their weapons over to such a super-government has been underway in school books and other places for a number of years.

In Magruder's *American Government* (1951), the student is told:

> We know that unity of our own States brought peace and strength to our country. We believe that similar cooperation will bring peace and good will to the nations of the world (pg 1) . . . When we have definite international laws and an army to enforce them we shall have international peace. When atomic bombs are made only by a world government and used only by a world army, who could resist? (pg 14)

Note the emphasis on "peace." The Scriptures say that the Anti-Christ "shall come in peaceably" and "by peace shall destroy many." How will he gain this power? The

Scripture says that he will "obtain the kingdom by flatteries." The final chapter of Magruder's book tells the student . . .

> . . . every thoughtful person looks to the United Nations as the best instrument for peace and world-wide security (pg 721)

Do you want to be considered to be "a thoughtful person?" Succumb to the *flattery* and support a United Nations army. Magruder tells the student that for the ultimate world government to work . . .

> . . . international commerce should be regulated . . . and international police, controlling all bombers, tanks, and armed vessels, and stronger than any probable grouping of nations, would enable nations to disarm with safety . . . But can we afford to pay taxes for support of an international organization? If an international police force can maintain peace, the member countries could save many times the cost of such an organization. (pgs 715-717)

If the "police force" controlled all the weapons, the nations would afford it — or else.

Would the American people buy the idea of turning their military forces over to the United Nations? What has the UN accomplished? Where has it kept the peace?

Many persons 35 years of age and younger believe that the United Nations won World War II and saved us from Hitler, Togo, and Mussolini. They believe it because history books have been rewritten to teach them so. *History of America* by Southworth is an eighth grade history which has been in use in many American schools since 1951. The text tells how when the great invasion force was assembled in England to assault Hitler's Europe . . .

> General Dwight Eisenhower of the United States Army came from the Italian front to command this mighty new United Nations force. (pg 769)

Captions on the photographs show "United Nations troops going ashore on D-Day" and "The United Nations beachhead on the French Coast." There is only one thing wrong with the story. D-Day, when Allied forces landed on the French Coast, was June 6, 1944. The United Nations was founded at San Francisco at a conference which opened on April 25, 1945 — ten months after the D-Day invasion.

The war in the Pacific is pictured similarly. The student who has been thus taught that the United Nations protected

America from Nazism and Mussolini's Fascism, would see nothing wrong with looking to the U.N. to protect the nation from communism as well. Pro-U.N. propaganda is built on deceit. The Scriptures say that the Anti-Christ "shall work deceitfully."

HIS REIGN

The Anti-Christ will reign for a period of seven years. The last three-and-a-half years will be a time of famine, pestilence, and terrible persecution for all who will not worship him as God. Great multitudes of Jews and Gentiles will be slain in the bloodiest period the world has ever known. Conditions will grow worse and worse. Finally, Jesus Christ will come back to defeat Satan and his forces in the battle of Armageddon. Before he comes, however, at least one-fourth of the earth's population will perish of hunger, the sword, and pestilence (Revelation 6:8). This could mean 750-million deaths in less than half a dozen years!

Satan has been working down through history to gain control of the world. When will he succeed? The Apostle Paul told of his efforts — and what has kept him from succeeding already — when he wrote:

> For the mystery of iniquity doth already work: only he who now hindereth will hinder, until he be taken out of the way. (II Thessalonians 2:7)

He who has "hindered" is the Holy Spirit of God. God's Spirit has been working through redeemed men down through the ages to restrain Satan and hold back the forces of evil. Satan will not triumph and the Anti-Christ will not come to power "until he (The Holy Spirit) be taken out of the way." This will happen when God takes those through whom the Holy Spirit works (all the saved believers) out of the world. St. Paul described this event when he wrote:

> For the Lord himself shall descend from heaven with a shout, with the voice of the archangel, and with the trump of God: and the dead in Christ shall rise first:
> Then we which are alive and remain shall be caught up together with them in the clouds, to meet the Lord in the air: and so shall we ever be with the Lord. (I Thessalonians 4:16-17)

Once the church (the body of true believers) is taken out of the world, "Then," St. Paul says, "shall that Wicked

One be revealed . . . even him, whose coming is after the working of Satan with all powers and signs and lying wonders." With the *true church* (all saved believers) gone, the False Prophet will rule over the harlot one-world ecumenical church described in Revelation 17 and 18. This false church will worship the Anti-Christ. After the seven year reign of Satan's Anti-Christ and False Prophet (during which the saved are in heaven with Jesus), Jesus Christ will personally return for the Battle of Armageddon. The Scriptures tell us:

> Behold, the Lord cometh with ten thousands of his saints, to execute judgment upon all, and to convince all that are ungodly among them of all their ungodly deeds which they have ungodly committed, and of all their hard speeches which ungodly sinners have spoken against him. (Jude 14-15)

And then the saints — the believers — shall "reign with Christ a thousand years." (Revelation 20:4)

THE SIGNS OF HIS COMING

When are all these things going to happen?

Is there any way of knowing if world events now unfolding are a definite forerunner of the personal return of Jesus Christ?

These are questions which have intrigued men down through the ages. Our Lord's disciples asked Him these questions even before He went to the Cross. They came to Him privately, saying:

> Tell us, when shall these things be? and what shall be the sign of thy coming, and of the end of the age? (Matthew 24:3)

In His answer Jesus said . . .

> . . . of that day and hour knoweth no man . . . But as the days of Noe [Noah] were, so shall also the coming of the Son of Man be. For as in the days that were before the flood they were eating and drinking, marrying and giving in marriage, until the day that Noe entered into the ark, and knew not until the flood came, and took them all away; so shall also the coming of the Son of Man be . . .
>
> Likewise also as it was in the days of Lot; they did eat, they drank, they bought, they sold, they planted, they builded; But the same day that Lot went out of Sodom it rained fire and brimstone from Heaven and destroyed them all.

Even thus shall it be in the day when the Son of Man
is revealed. (Matthew 24:36-39, Luke 17:28-30)

There is much to be learned from these few words of
Jesus Christ which point us to the days of Noah and Lot.
God has given us much significant information about conditions and characteristics in those days. The days of Noah
and the days of Lot were days of "business as usual." Pleasure, things of the family, and commerce occupied almost
all men. God warned men, through the preaching of Enoch
and Noah of judgment to come. Almost all, however, were
too busy enjoying themselves to listen. Then, one day, judgment fell. The only ones who escaped were the mere handful who had heeded God's warnings. So shall it be, Jesus
said, in the day of the coming of the Son of man. Are we
nearing that day? Are men today so wrapped up in business,
pleasure and family that they never heed warnings from
God's Word?

The days of Noah were also days of violence. The Scriptures tell us:

> The earth also was corrupt before God, and the earth was
> filled with violence . . . And God saith unto Noah, The end
> of all flesh is come before me: for the earth is *filled with*
> *violence* . . . (Genesis 6:11, 13)

The earth today is *filled with violence* as never before.
In America, snipers operate in the streets of major cities.
Senseless crimes of *violence* against people such as assault,
rape, mugging, and murder are the fastest growing categories
of crime. No period in human history has been so marked
by mass murder, liquidation and genocide as the last 50
years have been. Communism has adopted terror and violence as a standard procedure. "As it was in the days of
Noah," Jesus said, "so shall it be in the days of the coming
of the Son of man."

The days of Noah were days of "marrying and giving in
marriage." They were days of bigamy. In the days before
the flood we find the first record of dual marriage, when . . .

> . . . Lamech said unto his wives, Adah and Zillah, Hear
> my voice; ye wives of Lamech, hearken unto my speech . . .
> (Genesis 4:23)

Today is also a day of bigamy. While men rarely marry
more than one woman at a time, they collect whole strings
of them — one at a time. This is bigamy in God's sight. In

1900, less than one out of 50 marriages ended in divorce. Today, one of three marriages end up in the courts. Jesus said, "As it was in the days of Noah, so shall it be in the day of the coming of the Son of man."

The days of Noah — the days before the flood — were days of religious apostasy. Cain was the first apostate. He decided he could worship God in his own way rather than the way God had proscribed. Today is a day of religious apostasy as well. *Newsweek*, on June 26, 1967, published the results of a survey made by the National Council of Churches of the voting delegates, alternates and accredited visitors to its 1966 General Assembly. The results showed that among these leaders of America's largest Protestant denominations . . .

> . . . over one-third could not state they have a firm belief in God . . . over 40% do not believe Jesus was divine . . . of those who do claim to believe in God, only one in four believes in a God powerful enough to have performed such Bible miracles as the Virgin Birth . . . only one in six accept the Bible doctrine of man's sinful nature. Slightly more than 60% of the delegates look forward to a life after death.[3]

The days of Noah were days of religious apostasy. So shall it be in the day of the coming of the Son of man.

The days of Lot in Sodom and Gomorrah were days of great productivity. High production resulted in material well-being, "pride" in their own accomplishments, "a fullness of bread," and an "abundance of idleness." God condemned each of these by-products of great material abundance as sin. (Ezekiel 16:49). The material well-being and "abundance of idleness" was coupled with a religious apostasy which removed the restraints from society. This resulted in the widespread sexual immorality for which the days of Lot are remembered today. The same conditions are producing a sexual revolution in America today. As was reported in detail earlier, statistics, surveys, and special studies show that in America since 1960 . . .

> . . . one out of four brides have been pregnant at the altar . . . half of all college girls have premarital sexual relations . . . big city high schools have opened special centers for pregnant students to continue schooling because of a 40% rise in pregnancies among unmarried teenagers . . . public health officials warn of a 255% increase in venereal diseases among teenagers.[4]

As it was in the days of Lot, so shall it be in the day when the Son of man is revealed.

The days of Lot, of course, typify something worse than "normal" sexual immorality. Sodom and Gomorrah were centers of perversion and rampant homosexuality. When two angels of God came to Sodom to warn Lot of the Judgment which was to fall on the city, Lot invited them to spend the night in his home. But . . .

> . . . before they lay down, the men of the city, even the men of Sodom, compassed the house round, both old and young, all the people from every quarter.
> And they called unto Lot, and said unto him, Where are the men which came in unto thee this night? bring them out unto us, that we may know them. (Genesis 19:4-5)

The context shows the way in which the men of Sodom wanted to "know" the men. Such homosexuality has been a problem in all ages. In Sodom it became socially acceptable among the leaders of society and the people — as it is becoming in the world today. Consider these facts:[5]

> A group of clergymen in San Francisco sponsored a dance for homosexuals and angrily assailed police who broke up the orgy . . . The English Parliament repealed laws prohibiting homosexual relations between consenting males . . . a Catholic priest in Holland "married" two males at mass . . .

> Ninety Episcopal priests participating in a conference sponsored by the Episcopal Dioceses of New York, Connecticut, Long Island and Newark agreed generally that the church should classify homosexual acts between consenting adults as "morally neutral." They acknowledged that in some cases such acts may even be a good thing "where participants are expressing genuine love."

> Opposing an effort to deport immigrants who are homosexuals on the grounds that they are not of "good moral character" Supreme Court Justice William O. Douglas wrote, "It is common knowledge that in this century homosexuals have risen high in our own public service — both in Congress and the executive branch — and have served with distinction."

Not only is homosexuality a problem in America — but it is condoned and encouraged by the leaders of society. Jesus said, "As it was in the days of Lot . . . even thus shall it be in the day when the Son of man is revealed." The final depths of sin and degradation into which Lot fell was revealed by his reaction when the men of the city

demanded that he turn over his male guests for their use.
Lot gave the mob an alternative. He said:

> I pray you, brethren, do not so wickedly. Behold now,
> I have two daughters which have not yet known man; let
> me, I pray you, bring them out to you, and do ye to them
> as it is good in your eyes: only unto these men do nothing
> (Genesis 19:7-8).

Lot's willingness to turn his daughters over to the mob
for their use is at the depth of degradation to which a
man can fall. What is the attitude of modern parents? An
insight comes from an article in the November 1967 *Redbook* magazine by a young mother. She wrote on "Why
I Believe In Sex Before Marriage." She said:

> I feel that young adult couples — and I stress adult — who
> have a healthy attitude toward sex can benefit greatly
> from a premarital relationship . . . I hope to bring my
> daughters up to share my ideas.

In April 1967, a Baltimore hospital announced that it. . .

> . . . provides birth control pills for the unmarried high
> school girl who is sexually involved with a number of boys
> or for the girl who is often intimate with her steady boy
> friend . . . Many of the girls are enrolled in the program by
> their parents. All must have parental consent to receive the
> pills.[6]

God's judgment fell on Sodom and Gomorrah for their
wickedness. America is going to be judged just as certainly.
The Lord gave His disciples many other signs of the
end of the age and of His personal return. Jesus told them. . .

> . . . ye shall hear of wars and rumors of wars . . . nation
> shall rise against nation . . . there shall be famines, and
> pestilences, and earthquakes, in divers places. All these are
> the beginning of sorrows (tribulation) . . . many false
> prophets shall arise and deceive many . . . because sin shall
> abound, the love of many shall wax cold . . . and this
> gospel of the kingdom shall be preached in all of the
> world . . . and then the end shall come.
> When therefore ye shall see the abomination of desola-
> tion, spoken of by Daniel the prophet, stand in the holy
> place, (whoso readeth, let him understand;) Then let them
> which be in Judea flee into the mountains . . . For then
> shall be great tribulation, such as was not since the beginning
> of the world to this time, no, nor shall ever be. (Matthew
> 24:4-21)

Many of these conditions have prevailed since Jesus went to Heaven nearly 2000 years ago. For this reason, men have always been looking for Him to return at any time. All that has characterized this age — war, famine, pestilence, sin, false prophets, persecution of the Jews, etc., — will be concentrated in awful intensity at the end of the age, for they are "the beginning of sorrows." For example, there has rarely been a time in history when some place in the world wasn't suffering from famine. However, there is now, for the first time, a real prospect of worldwide famine. During 1966 newspapers carried these headlines:

> World Pantry Getting Bare, Says F.A.O. . . . Surpluses Gone — Food Crisis Coming . . . Threat Of World Food Crisis Spurs Farm Policy Debate . . . Hunger Ahead, Populations Soar, Food Dwindles . . . Grain Surplus Declines, Storage Space Is Empty.

With the world's population expected to double by the end of the century, a U.N. agricultural expert said:

> No revolution in agricultural production that we can conceive of will bring adequate food supplies for a population expanding at this rate. The resources of this earth can scarcely cope with this now.[7]

World-wide famine is now a possibility. The other "signs" are being fulfilled also. In fact, only one of the signs Jesus mentioned as preceding His coming could not conceivably be construed to have been fulfilled. He said:

> When therefore ye shall see the abomination of desolation, spoken of by Daniel the Prophet, stand in the holy place, (whoso readeth, let him understand;) Then let them which be in Judea flee into the mountains . . . (Matthew 24:15-16)

The "abomination of desolation" spoken of by Daniel the Prophet is the Anti-Christ. The "holy place" where he is to stand in the Temple in Jerusalem. Since 70 A.D. there has been no Temple — and the Jews have not even controlled the site of the Temple so as to be able to start rebuilding it. However, in the six day war in June 1967, Israel recaptured the site on which the Temple is to be rebuilt.

Time magazine quoted Jewish historian Israel Eldad on plans for rebuilding the Temple. He said, "We are at the stage where David was when he liberated Jerusalem. From that time until the construction of the Temple by

Solomon, only one generation passed. So will it be with us."[8]

Actual construction on the Temple need not be a generation away. Solomon spent seven years building the original.[9] It could be rebuilt in a much shorter time with modern construction methods — particularly if reports which have circulated for years are true. According to these recurring reports most of the construction materials have been lovingly prepared and prefabricated by Jews in all parts of the world. They are now awaiting shipment back to Israel for assembly.

As the Anti-Christ will not "stand in the holy place" until midway in the seven year tribulation period, the Temple does not need to be rebuilt before God takes His church (body of saved people) out of the world. When that happens, Satan can bring the Anti-Christ and the False Prophet to power. They can complete the job of establishing the one-world church and one-world government . . . and rebuilding the Temple.

WHAT WILL THIS MEAN TO THE INDIVIDUAL?

When Jesus Christ comes for His saints, this last great drama of this age will begin to unfold. What will it mean for the Christian? What will happen to the unsaved Jew? What about the unsaved Gentile? What would it mean for you? The Scriptures provide definite answers.

For the Christian, a clue is found in the Lord's Words — "as it was in the days of Noah." There was a man named Enoch who lived before the flood. His life — and God's dealing with him — typify what will happen to Christians before the end of this age. Of Enoch, the Scriptures say:

> And Enoch lived sixty and five years, and begat Methuselah: And Enoch walked with God after he begat Methuselah three hundred years, and begat sons and daughters: And all the days of Enoch were three hundred sixty and five years: And Enoch walked with God: and he was not: for God took him. (Genesis 5:21-23)

The lives of each of the other men who are described in the 5th Chapter of Genesis, conclude, ". . . and he died." This was not said about Enoch, for he did not die. The New Testament says:

> By faith, Enoch was translated that he should not see

death: and was not found, because God had translated him:
for before his translation he had this testimony, that he
pleased God. (Hebrews 11:5)

God took Enoch directly to Heaven "in the twinkling of
an eye." Jesus said, "As it was in the days of Noah, so
shall it be in the day of the coming of the Son of man."
When the end of this age comes, the born-again believer
will not die either. He will be caught up in Heaven just
as Enoch was. As St. Paul wrote:

> For the Lord himself shall descend from Heaven with
> a shout, with the voice of the archangel, and with the trump
> of God: and the dead in Christ shall rise first:
> Then we which are alive and remain shall be caught up
> together with them in the clouds, to meet the Lord in
> the air: and so shall we ever be with the Lord. (I
> Thessalonians 4:16-17)

WHAT WILL CHRIST'S COMING
MEAN TO THE JEW?

Once the born-again believers are translated into the
presence and safety of Jesus Christ in Heaven, Satan's
last restraints will be removed. Those left in the world —
Jew and Gentile — will undergo seven years of the worst
tribulation the world has ever known.

For the Jew, Daniel the Prophet wrote:

> . . . there shall be a time of trouble, such as never was
> since there was a nation even to that same time. (Daniel
> 12:1)

This will be the "time of Jacob's trouble" of which other
Scriptures prophecy. During this time of great and terrible
tribulation, all the nations of the earth will be arrayed
against Israel. The Lord, speaking through Zechariah has
promised that the time of trouble will culminate when . . .

> . . . I will gather all nations against Jerusalem to battle;
> and the city shall be taken, and the houses rifled, and the
> women ravished; and half of the city shall go into captivity,
> and the residue of the people shall not be cut off from
> the city.
> Then shall the Lord go forth, and fight against those
> nations, as when he fought in the day of battle. And his
> feet shall stand upon the Mount of Olives, which is before
> Jerusalem on the east . . . (Zechariah 14:2-4)

Before the Lord returns, however, two-thirds of the Jews will have worshipped the Anti-Christ. They will die from pestilence, famine, persecution, and the sword. Zechariah wrote:

> And it shall come to pass, that in all the land, saith the Lord, two parts therein shall be cut off and die; but the third shall be left therein.
> And I will bring the third part through the fire, and will refine them as silver is refined, and will try them as gold is tried; they shall call on my name, and I will hear them: I will say, it is my people: and they shall say, The Lord is my God. (Zechariah 13:8-9)

The prophecies of what will happen when Jesus returns to defeat Satan and his forces are fantastically detailed. Over 500 years before Christ came the *first* time, God speaking through Zechariah promised:

> . . . I will pour upon the house of David, and upon the inhabitants of Jerusalem, the spirit of grace and of supplications: and they shall look upon me whom they pierced, and they shall mourn for him, as one mourneth for his only son, and shall be in bitterness for him, as one that is in bitterness for his firstborn . . .
> And one shall say unto him, What are these wounds in thine hands? Then he shall answer, Those with which I was wounded in the house of my friends. (Zechariah 12:10, 13:6)

Following the Lord's return, this believing remnant of Israel which survives the terrible tribulation and turns to Jesus Christ shall enter his kingdom and live under His rule for 1000 years.

THE UNSAVED GENTILES

Great multitudes of Gentiles *who never heard the Gospel of Jesus Christ during this age* will also be saved during the tribulation period. They will hear the good news that Jesus died for them from the lips of the 144,000 Jewish preachers God will raise up. Many of these will be martyred because of their faith in Jesus and for refusing to worship the Anti-Christ.

No Gentile reader of this book will be included in this group which will be saved during the tribulation. Those who have been born again by trusting the shed blood of Jesus Christ will spend the tribulation period in Heaven with Jesus. Those who have heard (or read) the Gospel during this present age have a terrible fate awaiting them if they refuse to accept Christ. They will be left behind when the born again believers are taken out of the world. Then, St. Paul writes . . .

> . . . shall that Wicked One be revealed . . . even him whose coming is after the working of Satan with all power and signs and lying wonders. And with all deceivableness of unrighteousness in them that perish; because they received not the love of the truth, that they might be saved.
>
> And for this cause God shall send them strong delusion, that they should believe a lie: That they all might be damned who believed not the truth but had pleasure in unrighteousness. (II Thessalonians 2:8-12)

God will permit the Anti-Christ to deceive all those who did not accept the gift of salvation when it was offered to them in this age. They will believe the lie that the Anti-Christ is the true God. For worshipping him, they will be damned forever. The deluded, who will believe the lie and will be condemned to hell for it, will include many drunkards, liars, and adulterers. Many "good" people who never thought they were bad enough to need a Saviour will also believe the lie and perish.

WHAT IF IT IS TODAY?

If Jesus Christ were to come tonight to take His born again believers out of this world, would you be among those left behind to believe a lie and be damned? Jesus said:

> For as in the days that were before the flood they were eating and drinking, marrying and giving in marriage, until the day that Noe entered the ark, and knew not until the flood came, and took them all away; so also shall the coming of the Son of man be.
>
> Then shall two be in the field; the one shall be taken, and the other left. Two women shall be grinding at the mill: the one shall be taken, and the other left . . .
>
> Therefore be ye also ready; for in such an hour as ye think not the Son of man cometh. (Matthew 24:38-41, 44)

How can you know if you are ready? Is there any way man can be certain of salvation? God's Word tells us that there is — and God wants us to know. The Apostle John wrote:

And this is the record, that God hath given to us eternal life, and this life is in his Son. He that hath the Son hath life; and he that hath not the Son of God hath not life. These things have I written unto you that *ye may know that ye have eternal life.* (I John 5:11-13)

Have you ever asked Jesus Christ to come into your heart to be *your* Saviour? If you have, you have eternal life and *are* saved, for *He promises:*

I will never leave thee, nor foresake thee. (Hebrews 13:5)

Once you have been saved, Jesus Christ will keep you saved, for He has been charged with this responsibility by His Father. He said:

. . . him that cometh to me I will in no wise cast out. For I came down from heaven, not to do mine own will, but the will of him that sent me. And this is the will of him that sent me, that of all which he hath given me I should lose nothing, but should raise it up again at the last day. (John 6:37-40)

We can't save ourselves, nor can we keep ourselves saved — but Christ will do it all.

WHAT CAN WE DO?

If the end of the age is near, do we have any responsibility other than getting right with God and watching for his return? If all these things are prophesied, why should we worry? If we oppose communism and world government and the one-world church when they are prophesied, aren't we really opposing God's plan for this age?

These are attitudes assumed by many sincere born-again Christians. But they are not Biblical positions for the end of the age. In I Thessalonians 1:9-10, the Apostle Paul outlines man's responsibility to God *for every age.* Paul shows that man is to . . .

. . . turn to God from idols to serve the living and true God; and to wait for his Son from heaven, whom he raised from the dead even Jesus, which delivered us from the wrath to come.

There is only one way to God and salvation for the Jew or Gentile — and that is by believing the Gospel. The Apostle Paul wrote:

For I am not ashamed of the gospel of Christ: for it is

the power of God unto salvation to *everyone that believeth:* to the Jew first and also to the Greek (Gentile). (Romans 1:16)

Moreover, brethren, I declare unto you the gospel which I preached unto you, which also ye have received, and wherein ye stand: By which also ye *are* saved.

. . . how that Christ died for our sins according to the scriptures; And that he was buried, and that he rose again the third day according to the scriptures. (I Corinthians 15:1-4)

Salvation is a gift from God. Anything which keeps you from asking for it and receiving it by faith is an "idol" from which you need to turn.

God saves those who believe so that they might serve Him — the living and true God. We serve Him as we . . .

. . . render to Caesar the things that are Caesar's, and to God the things that are God's. (Mark 12:17)

Born-again people who have turned to God who are serving Him daily can watch and wait with joy and anticipation for His Son from Heaven. They have the Lord's promise that they will be delivered from the wrath to come.

The troubles of this age stem from born again Christians who are complacently sitting back watching and waiting for Jesus to come. They've decided that since the end of the age is near, no real revival is possible. Satan has also convinced them that to fight communism, one-world government and the apostate church is to fight God's plan for the age. They go wrong three ways:

The end of the age seems near — but it is not certain. For over 2000 years men have looked for the imminent return of Jesus. In Thessalonica men became so certain that Jesus would return before winter that they failed to plant their fields. Paul was forced to warn them, "For even when we were with you, this we commanded you, that if any would not work, neither should he eat."

Jesus commanded that we continue to work. Before He went to Heaven, He told His followers:

Occupy till I come . . . Blessed is that servant, whom his lord when he cometh shall find so doing. (Luke 19:10; Matthew 25:46)

Jesus did not say, "Occupy till it looks like I am about to come. . . ." but rather, "Occupy till I come." The only thing which has kept Satan from carrying out his program for world domination during the last 2000 years has been God's Holy Spirit working *through* believers to restrain him. For the Holy Spirit to work, the believer's life must be yielded to God.

Believers go wrong and forget "to serve the living and true God" because they know their salvation is certain. They forget that when Jesus does return they will immediately go before Him for judgment. St. Paul told the believers at Corinth:

> . . . we must all appear before the judgment seat of Christ that everyone may receive the things done in his body, according to that he hath done, whether it be good or bad. (II Corinthians 5:10)

This judgment has nothing to do with *where* the born-again believer will be in eternity. That is settled, once and for all, when he trusts the shed blood of Christ as the satisfaction of all punishment due for his sins. Jesus promised:

> Verily, verily, I say unto you, He that heareth my word, and believeth on him that sent me, *hath* everlasting life, *and shall not come into condemnation;* but is passed from death unto life. (John 5:24)

At the judgment seat of Jesus Christ, every *believer* will answer to his Saviour for how faithfully he served the living and true God. On that great and glorious day every believer will receive rewards for those things done in the power of the Holy Spirit for Jesus Christ. And we will also be required to answer to our Lord for all the time we satisfied self in the power of the flesh. If you are a born-again believer, what would happen if He came today and you had to stand before His judgment seat? Ask yourself . . .

> . . . How many of your friends, relatives, children and loved ones would be left behind to worship the Anti-Christ because you didn't care enough — or were too embarrassed — to preach, plead, and pray for their salvation?

> . . . How would you explain to the Lord why you never really let His life show in yours? Why did you never let it show on the job, in school, or in the neighborhood that you were indeed "a new creature in Christ?" Has whatever witness you had as a Christian carried very little weight with the unsaved because you never showed you were different?

If you have refused to obey God's clear scriptural commands to come out of an unbelieving church which no longer preaches the whole counsel of God how will your excuses sound in His presence?

These are some of the things we are to "render unto God." We will also have to answer to Jesus Christ for those things we were to "render unto Caesar." Ask yourself:

Have you fulfilled your responsibility to make our God-given form of self-government work? What part have you played in making your political party work?

When Jesus Christ examines your efforts to "resist the devil" and his communist stooges how will your efforts (or excuses) stack up? Have you informed yourself? Have you worked to alert and educate others? Have you supported and helped others who are doing this work?

All of us fall short — that's why we need a Saviour. However, Christians of this generation will have much to answer for at the judgment seat of Jesus Christ. His judgment seat will be a fearsome place for the carnal Christian for there, the Scriptures tell us . . .

. . . Every man's work shall be made manifest: for the day shall declare it, because it shall be revealed by fire; and the fire shall try every man's work of what sort it is.

If any man's work abide which he has built thereupon, he shall receive a reward. If any man's work shall be burned, he shall suffer loss: but he himself shall be saved; yet so as by fire. (I Corinthians 3:13-15)

How will your works for God *and* Country measure up in that day?

What Can You Do?

> *Truly in vain is salvation hoped for from the hills, and from the multitude of mountains: truly in the Lord our God is the salvation of Israel.*
>
> — *Jeremiah 3:23*

WHEN THE BOOK *None Dare Call It Treason* was published in 1964, its last chapter closed with a call for "a spiritual commitment." J. Edgar Hoover was quoted as saying that while the fight against communism was being fought on economic, psychological, diplomatic, and military fronts, that the battle, at its heart, was a spiritual one.

As the author, I admonished each reader to "examine your own personal religious beliefs," and asked the question, "Is God a meaningful, consuming force in your life?"

At that point, God was not "a meaningful, consuming force" to me because I had never accepted His gift of salvation. I thought I was a Christian. From my childhood, I had been active in the work of the church. I edited a church paper for a time. As a layman, I had spoken from the pulpits of a number of good churches — yet I had never really become a Christian *in the Bible sense of the word.*

On February 19, 1965, I came to see that in spite of my "good" life and church affiliations I was a sinner who deserved to go to hell. At that point, the words, "Christ died for our sins," which I had always believed *in my head* became very real — and very important — to me. About 2:30 am the next morning in the dark living room of my home, I asked God to forgive my sins *on the basis that I believed Christ had already taken all my punishment.* Although, I wasn't consciously making "a spiritual decision" that night, Jesus Christ came into my heart and became my Saviour. It was almost a week, however, before I realized what had happened to me.

Since that time, God has made a new person of me, doing things in my life and heart I was never able to do for myself. The Bible now makes sense to me. It's alive and real and I want to read it. Prayer is a joyous time of communion with the God of this universe instead of a duty to be fulfilled. I look forward to going to church to hear God's Word preached. Most important, I long to tell people about what Jesus has done for me — and what He will do for them. In short, He has fulfilled in these and a thousand other ways the words of St. Paul who wrote . . .

> . . . if any man be in Christ, he is a new creature: old things are passed away: behold all things are become new. And all things are of God . . . (II Corinthians 5:17-18a)

Because of what God has done in my heart and life in the last three years, I know that He can do anything. I know that the answer to America's serious problems will be found only if our country returns to the place where it is truly "one nation under God" again. This new book, which brings *None Dare Call It Treason* up to date, reflects this knowledge.

America is in deep trouble. The Bible, the lessons of history, and the words of General MacArthur all testify that unless America turns back to God, she is doomed. Nations, of course, don't awaken spiritually. Only individuals do.

Are you willing to have the spiritual awakening which can save America start in *your* heart? If you have never definitely accepted God's gift of salvation and eternal life, will you do it now? Read the prayer printed below. If you believe it *without reservation* and want Jesus Christ to be *your* Saviour, sign your name in the space provided:

> I know that I am a sinner who deserves to go to Hell. I know that I cannot save myself. I believe that God, in the person of Jesus Christ, suffered and died as my substitute on the cross of Calvary. Because the punishment I deserve is fully satisfied, I am now asking for and receiving forgiveness of my sins. I believe that Jesus rose from the dead and I want Him to come into my heart now to be my Saviour, Lord and Master.

Signed: ....

Now that you have been saved Satan will try to make you doubt. Your own feelings will change from day-to-day. God's Word, however, never changes. He promises:

Whosoever shall call on the name of the Lord, *shall* be saved . . . him that cometh to me I will in no wise cast out. (Romans 10:13, John 6:37)

Now that you have accepted God's gift of salvation, you need to tell others. Early in His ministry Jesus saved a man and then commanded: "Go home to thy friends and tell them how great things the Lord hath done for thee. . ." As you tell your wife, friends, co-workers, etc. that Jesus saved you, your salvation will become even more real to you — and you will be taking your first steps as a witness for Him. Write to me — John Stormer, Box 32, Florissant, Mo. — so I can rejoice with you. I'll send you a note of encouragement and a little booklet to help you start living your new life in Christ.

Now that Jesus Christ has saved you, reread Chapter IX — and then go to work in His strength to save your country.

Yours for Christ and Country
John A. Stormer

He Can Do It

By the word of the Lord were the heavens made; and all the host of them by the breath of his mouth.

He gathereth the waters of the sea together as an heap: he layeth up the depth in storehouses.

Let all the earth fear the Lord: let all the inhabitants of the world stand in awe of him.

For he spake, and it was done; he commanded, and it stood fast.

The Lord bringeth the counsel of the heathen to nought: he maketh the devices of the people of none effect.

The counsel of the Lord standeth forever, the thoughts of his heart to all generations.

Blessed is the nation whose God is the Lord; and the people whom he hath chosen for his inheritance. (Psalm 33:6-12)

REFERENCES

Chapter I

1 Speech, J. Edgar Hoover, New York City, Dec. 14, 1963
2 Table, U.S. Casualties in Major Wars, Information Please Almanac, 1958, Pg. 414
3 AP, St. Louis Globe Democrat, Jul. 29, 1965
4 St. Louis Globe Democrat, Oct. 19, 1965; Feb. 21, 1966; Mar. 21, 1966; Jan. 12, 1964; Minneapolis Tribune, Sep. 29, 1966; St. Louis Post Dispatch, Aug. 9, 1967
5 St. Louis Post Dispatch, Jan. 23, 1967; AP, Buffalo Courier Express, Dec. 12, 1967
6 AP, St. Louis Globe Democrat, Mar. 17, 1967; J. Edgar Hoover, House Subcommittee on Appropriations, Mar. 4, 1965; pg. 67-69
7 Ibid., Apr. 26, 1967
8 Congressional Record, Nov. 8, 1967
9 See Chapter IV
10 Congressional Record, Jul. 18, 1967
11 St. Louis Post Dispatch, Jul. 18, 1967
12 St. Louis Globe Democrat, Nov. 19, 1965
13 St. Louis Post Dispatch, Aug. 10, 1967
14 St. Louis Post Dispatch, Nov. 12, 1967
15 None Dare Call It Treason, pg. 12, 29, 57, 90, 118
16 Ibid., pg. 12, 29-31, 39, 45, 51, 56-57, 179, 221
17 See Chapter IV
18 See Chapter V
19 Reader's Digest, Jul. 1966, pg. 71
20 Ibid., Aug. 1966, pg. 131
21 Ibid.
22 AP, St. Louis Globe Democrat, Feb. 1, 1968
23 1968 State Of The Union Message
24 St. Louis Post Dispatch, Jul. 15, 1965
25 Stormer, None Dare Call It Treason, pg. 220
26 Bakewell, Thirteen Curious Errors About Money, pg. 10
27 Stormer, None Dare Call It Treason, pg. 220-21
28 The Reader's Digest, Aug. 1966, pg. 132
29 See Chapter VI
30 FBI Law Enforcement Bulletin, Feb. 1967
31 Reader's Digest, May 1964
32 The Star, Yorba Linda, Calif., Nov. 15, 1967
33 Preliminary Report of Investigating Committee, Senator James E. Whetmore, Jan. 25, 1968, pg. 4
34 Ibid., pg. 3-4
35 Press Release, Senator John Schmitz, 34th District, California, Nov. 28, 1967
36 See Chapter V
37 Magruder, American Government, pg. 13

Chapter II

1 Testimony, Hoover, House Appropriation Subcommittee, Feb. 16, 1967, pg. 619
2 New York Times, Jul. 22, 1964
3 Luce, Road To Revolution, pg. 9
4 Ibid.
5 Report of Cuyahoga County Special Grand Jury, Aug. 9, 1966
6 Quoted by Hoover, Statement, 17th Nat. Conv. CPUSA, SISS, Jan. 26, 1960, pg. 6
7 Ibid., pg. 7
8 Testimony, Hoover, House Appropriations Subcommittee, Feb. 1967, pg. 619
9 Ibid., 1964, quoted U.S. News and World Report, May 4, 1965
10 Ibid., 1967, pg. 619
11 Cleveland Press, Oct. 24, 1967
12 AP, St. Louis Globe Democrat, Aug. 3, 1967
13 Ibid.
14 New York Post, Jun. 15, 1967
15 St. Louis Post Dispatch, Sep. 15, 1967
16 St. Louis Globe Democrat, Aug. 3, 1967
17 St. Louis Post Dispatch, Jul. 25, 1967
18 Ibid., Jul. 26, 1967
19 St. Louis Globe Democrat, Aug. 19, 1967
20 Ibid., Aug. 9, 1967
21 Ibid.
22 Ibid., Aug. 9-14, 1967, as distributed by North American Newspaper Alliance, Inc.
23 Ibid., Aug. 10, 1967
24 Ibid.
25 Ibid., Aug. 12, 1967
26 Ibid., Aug. 3, 1967
27 St. Louis Post Dispatch, Aug. 2, 1967
28 Ibid.
29 St. Louis Globe Democrat, Aug. 7, 1967
30 Human Events, Aug. 27, 1966
31 Ibid.
32 Ibid.
33 Ibid., Nov. 18, 1967
34 St. Louis Post Dispatch, Aug. 4, 1967
35 Ibid., Aug. 5, 1967
36 Human Events, Aug. 5, 1967

37 St. Louis Post Dispatch, Aug. 13, 1967, Louisville Courier Journal, Aug. 13, 1967
38 Ibid., Congressional Record, Feb. 8, 1967, pg. A544
39 Congressional Record, Feb. 8, 1967
40 Ibid., Nov. 14, 1967, pg. H15180
41 Ibid., pg. H15189
42 U.S. News & World Report, Jan. 31, 1966
43 Hearings, Inv. of Comm. Act. in St. Louis Area, HCUA, Jun. 5, 1966, pg. 4852-3
44 Human Events, Oct. 21, 1967
45 St. Louis Globe Democrat, Aug. 3, 1967
46 St. Louis Post Dispatch
47 Testimony, Hoover, House Appropriations Committee, Feb. 16, 1967, pg. 619
48 Statement, Hoover, The Communist Party Line, SISS, Sep. 23, 1961, pg. 5
49 Testimony, Hoover, House Appropriations Committee, Feb. 16, 1967, pg. 619
50 St. Louis Globe Democrat, Aug. 10, 1967
51 World Communist Movement, Selective Chronology, HCUA, 1960, pg. 101, 106-7

Chapter III

1 St. Louis Globe Democrat, Mar. 23, 1967
2 Ibid., Jan. 27, 1967
3 Ibid.
4 Ibid.
5 St. Louis Globe Democrat, Sep. 13, 1967
6 Ibid., Sep. 15, 1967
7 AP, Atlantic City Press, Jun. 29, 1967
8 St. Louis Globe Democrat, May 13, 1967
9 Ibid.
10 Ibid.
11 Ibid., Aug. 2, 1967
12 Ibid.
13 Hearings, Interlocking Subversion in Gov. Depts., SISS, 1954, pg. 1653-1708; 1711-33; 2019-46
14 Ibid.
15 St. Louis Globe Democrat, Mar. 23, 1967
16 Ibid., Jan. 27, 1967
17 AP, Atlantic City Press, Aug. 28, 1967
18 Donovan, Eisenhower, The Inside Story, pg. 126
19 AP, The Morning Herald, Durham, N.C., Jul. 14, 1966
20 Ibid.
21 Dallas Times Herald, May 19, 1967
22 St. Louis Globe Democrat, Feb. 6, 1968
23 St. Louis Globe Democrat, Jan. 12, 1968
24 Human Events, Oct. 23, 1965
25 Speech, Dean Rusk, International Union of Electrical, Radio and Machine workers, Washington, D.C., Feb. 25, 1964
26 St. Louis Globe Democrat, Mar. 21, 1966
27 Ibid.
28 Ibid., Jan. 12, 1968
29 St. Louis Globe Democrat, Apr. 14, 1966
30 Ibid., Mar. 31, 1966
31 Indianapolis News, Sep. 16, 1967
32 Human Events, Jul 22, 1967
33 Ibid., Nov. 25, 1967
34 Philadelphia Inquirer, Mar. 2, 1965
35 Congressional Record, Nov. 8, 1967
36 Stormer, None Dare Call It Treason, Chapter XIV

Chapter IV

1 Speech, Dean Rusk, World Affairs Conference, International Union of Electrical, Radio, and Machine Workers, Washington, D.C., Feb. 25, 1964
2 Partisan Review, May-June 1947, Cong. Record, Feb. 6, 1962, pg. A881-3
3 Ibid.
4 St. Louis Post Dispatch, Jan. 30, 1967
5 Ibid.
6 State of the Union message, Jan. 13, 1967
7 Atlantic City Press, Jun. 26, 1967
8 New York Times, Jun. 26, 1967
9 St. Louis Post Dispatch, Jan. 17, 1966
10 Ibid.
11 St. Louis Globe Democrat, Jan. 15, 1966
12 St. Louis Post Dispatch, Jan. 24, 1966
13 Philadelphia Daily News, Jul. 1, 1965
14 AP, St. Louis Globe Democrat, Jun. 8, 1966
15 Ibid., Jul. 20, 1965
16 Ibid., Jul. 17, 1965; St. Louis Post Dispatch, Dec. 14, 1965
17 St. Louis Post Dispatch, Dec. 14, 1965; Jun. 6, 1966
18 Dec. 14, 1965
19 U.S. News & World Report, Aug. 21, 1961
20 Crimes of Khrushchev, HCUA, Part I, pg. 7; Part II, pg. 2
21 For a complete discussion of the problem of communist infiltration into government and efforts to block investigations of such activities, see None Dare Call It Treason, pg. 37-47

22 Hearings, Institute of Pacific Relations, SISS, pg. 4777
23 Ibid., pg. 4776
24 See None Dare Call It Treason, pg. 12-13 for references

Chapter V

1 The American Legion Magazine, Nov. 1954, pg. 6
2 St. Louis Globe Democrat, Aug. 5, 1966
3 Ibid., Sep. 28, 1966
4 Ibid.
5 Ibid.
6 AP, Ibid., Mar. 30, 1967
7 Indianapolis Star, Sep. 20, 1967
8 St. Louis Post Dispatch, Apr. 18, 1967
9 Santa Barbara, Calif. News-Press, Aug. 24, 1967
10 St. Louis Globe Democrat, Sep. 4, 1967
11 Ibid.
12 Political Affairs, Aug. 1965
13 AP, St. Louis Globe Democrat, Nov. 25, 1965
14 Ibid., Mar. 31, 1967
15 New York Times, Dec. 12, 1966
16 This Week, Jan. 8, 1967
17 St. Louis Post Dispatch, Jan. 13, 1966
18 Spotlight on Youth, St. Louis Globe Democrat, Nov. 9, 1965
19 St. Louis Post Dispatch, May 27, 1967
20 The Sun-Sentinel, Pompano Beach, Fla., Feb. 17, 1967
21 New York Times, Nov. 30, 1967
22 Ibid.
23 Boston Globe, Dec. 12, 1967
24 Filmed testimony shown in movie, Red China Outlaw
25 St. Louis Globe Democrat, Oct. 6, 1966
26 AP, The Lima, Ohio News, Oct. 13, 1967
27 Cleveland Press, Oct. 24, 1967
28 AP, The Morning News, Erie, Pa., Dec. 5, 1966
29 Testimony, J. Edgar Hoover, House Appropriation Subcommittee, Mar. 4, 1965, pg. 43
30 Ibid., Feb. 16, 1967, pg. 37
31 The Sentinel, Orlando, Fla., Feb. 19, 1967
32 Testimony, J. Edgar Hoover, House Appropriations Subcommittee, Feb. 16, 1967, pg. 34
33 Reader's Digest, Mar. 1966
34 Smut: The Poison That Preys on Children, Good Housekeeping, Nov. 1961
35 Stormer, Florissant Times, May 22, 1963
36 Non-Military Warfare in Britain, Foreign Affairs Publ. Co., Ltd., 1966, pg. 5-6

37 Ibid., quoting Cinema Documents, The Italian Communist Party, Issue No. 12, pg. 224-5.
38 Military Cold War Education, Hearings, Senate Committee on Armed Services, Apr. 1962
39 Castro's Network in the U.S., Hearings, SISS, Part 6, Feb. 8, 1963, pg. 339-50
40 Ibid., pg. 366-9
41 Ibid., pg. 337
42 Redbook, Sep. 1965, pg. 57
43 Ibid.
44 Ibid., pg. 136
45 Philadelphia Evening Bulletin, Apr. 19, 1967
46 St. Louis Globe Democrat, Jun. 14, 1966
47 Ibid., This Week Magazine, Jan. 29, 1967
48 Redbook, Feb. 1967, pg. 68
49 Human Events, Aug. 27, 1966
50 Ibid.
51 Redbook, Nov. 1967, pg. 10
52 Cleveland Plain Dealer, Oct. 13, 1967
53 St. Louis Globe Democrat, Mar. 28, 1967
54 St. Louis Post Dispatch, Mar. 28, 1967
55 Ibid., May 11, 1967
56 1762 Edition
57 McGuffey's Fifth Eclectic Reader, New American Library Edition, pg. vii
58 Ibid., xii-xiii
59 St. Louis Globe Democrat, Sep. 28, 1966
60 Letter to ministers, NBC News, quoted The Evangelist, Highland Park Baptist Church, Chattanooga, Tenn., Jan. 1968

Chapter VI

1 Speech, J. Edgar Hoover, Valley Forge, Pa., Feb. 22, 1962
2 St. Louis Post Dispatch, Feb. 16, 1966
3 Ibid., Jul. 28, 1966
4 Ecumenical Press Service release, Apr. 26, 1967
5 Jones, Christ's Alternative To Communism, pg. 224; The Choice Before Us, pg. 133
6 UPI, Philadelphia Evening Bulletin, Mar. 15, 1966
7 Bennett, Foreign Policy in Christian Perspective, 1966, pg. 94
8 Ibid.
9 AP, The News and Observer, Raleigh, N.C., Jul. 17, 1966
10 St. Louis Post Dispatch, Feb. 23, 1966
11 AP, News and Observer, Raleigh, N.C., Jul. 17, 1966
12 The Crusader (American Baptist Convention), Dec. 1967
13 The Sword of the Lord, Jan. 12, 1968

14 Transcript published by Church League of America, Wheaton, Illinois
15 Seattle Times, Sep. 15, 1967; Seattle Post Intelligencer, Sep. 16, 1967
16 Seattle Times, Sep. 19, 1967
17 Hoover, Yearend Report To The Attorney General, quoted by The Wanderer, St. Paul, Minn., Jan. 18, 1968
18 Philadelphia Inquirer, Apr. 27, 1967
19 AP, The Leader, Corning, N.Y., Nov. 14, 1967
20 Pageant Magazine, Oct. 1965, pg. 46-47
21 Ibid., pg. 47
22 Ibid., pg. 50
23 New York Times, Nov. 29, 1967
24 pg. 6-7
25 pg. 5
26 Newsweek, Jun. 26, 1967, pg. 69
27 Issues Presented By The Air Reserve Training Manual, Hearings, HCUA, Feb. 25, 1960, p. 1303
28 Investigation of Communist Activities in the New York Area, Part 5, HCUA, 83rd Congress, 1st Session, pg. 2017
29 pg. 11
30 Hoover, A Study of Communism, pg. 88
31 Miami News, Dec. 5, 1962
32 St. Paul Dispatch, Sep. 28, 1966
33 Congressional Record, Feb. 6, 1962, pg. A882
34 pg. 23-24
35 pg. 27
36 pg. 134-135
37 Kennedy, God's Good News, pg. 125
38 Denver Post, Mar. 6, 1965
39 The Mindszenty Report, Oct. 15, 1967
40 Ibid.
41 Miami Herald, Feb. 16, 1967
42 Milwaukee Journal, Mar. 19, 1966
43 pg. 38
44 New York Times, Dec. 11, 1966
45 Grant, Basic Christian Beliefs, pg. 161
46 Congressional Record, Feb. 6, 1962, pg. A882
47 AP, Philadelphia Evening Bulletin, Nov. 19, 1965
48 Grant, Basic Christian Beliefs, pg. 69, 72
49 The Confession of 1967, The United Presbyterian Church in the U.S.A.
50 Otten, Baal or God, pg. 34

Chapter VII

1 Ryle, Five Christian Leaders, pg. 10-11
2 Robinson, Proofs Of A Conspiracy, 1798

3 Ryle, Five Christian Leaders, pg. 11
4 New York Times, Feb. 13, 1966
5 Letters of John Newton, pg. 7
6 Ryle, Five Christian Leaders, pg. 17
7 Ibid., pg. 17-18
8 Ibid., pg. 18
9 Burns, Revivals, Their Laws and Leaders, pg. 206-288
10 Introduction, Selected Sermons of George Whitefield, pg. 19
11 Cyclopedia of Biblical, Theological & Ecclesiastical Lectures, pg. 18
12 Quoted by Bready, This Freedom Whence?, pg. 95
13 Ibid., pg. 96-97
14 Ibid., pg. 97
15 St. Louis Post Dispatch, Feb. 17, 1966
16 Bready, This Freedom Whence?, pg. xv
17 Nation Under God, pg. 24
18 Ibid., pg. 25
19 Maxfield, Revival in America, pg. 283
20 Ibid.
21 Bready, This Freedom Whence?, pg. 342

Chapter VIII

1 Communist Persecution of Churches in Red China and Korea, HCUA, pg. 3
2 Ibid., pg. 4
3 Ibid., pg. 31
4 Ibid., pg. 31-32
5 Dooley, Deliver Us From Evil, pg. 98
6 Ibid.
7 Ibid., pg. 101
8 Quoted, Hoover, Masters of Deceit, pg. 184
9 UPI, Binghamton, N.Y. Sun Bulletin, Dec. 7, 1967
10 AP, St. Louis Post Dispatch, Nov. 19, 1967
11 Ibid., Jan. 9, 1967
12 The Blade, Toledo, Ohio, Oct. 14, 1966
13 St. Louis Post Dispatch, Aug. 24, 1966
14 Baptist Bible Tribune, Feb. 16, 1968
15 St. Louis Post Dispatch, Aug. 24, 1966
16 Ibid., Aug. 13, 1967

Chapter IX

1 See page
2 Orr, The Second Evangelical Awakening, pg. 11
3 Ibid., pg. 14-16
4 Ibid., pg. 76
5 Ibid., pg. 141
6 Bishop Warren Cander quoted by Orr, Ibid., pg. 95

7 Beardsley, History of American Revivals
8 Wirt, Sketches of the Life and Character of Patrick Henry, quoted by Jacobs, Little Known Stories from American History, pg. 143

Chapter X

1 UPI — Daily Bulletin, Anderson, Ind., Sep. 20, 1967
2 Document 7277, U.S. Department of State, Sep. 1961, pg. 18-19

3 Newsweek, Jun. 26, 1967
4 Indianapolis Star, Sep. 20, 1967; St. Louis Globe-Democrat, Sep. 28, 1966; New York Times, Dec. 12, 1966; This Week, Jan. 8, 1967
5 San Francisco Sunday Chronicle, Jan. 3, 1963; New York Times, Nov. 29, 1967; Human Events, Jun. 3, 1967
6 Philadelphia Evening Bulletin, Apr. 19, 1967
7 AP, Seattle Times, Nov. 14, 1966
8 Time, Jun. 30, 1967
9 I Kings 6:38

INDEX

AFL-CIO, 53

Anslinger, Commissioner Harry, 71

Aptheker, Bettina, 69

Aptheker, Herbert, 69

Ashbrook, Cong. John, 52

Associated Press, 44-45, 48, 71, 94, 136

Augustine, 112

Baldwin, James, 99

Baldwin, Stanley, 128

Baptist, 80, 136-37

Baptist Convention, Southern, 99

Baptist World Alliance, 137

Basic Christian Beliefs, 116-17

Beatles, 67

Bennett, Dr. John C., 92-94, 96, 101, 102, 120

Bentley, Elizabeth, 63

birth control pills, 79

Blake, Dr. Eugene Carson, 91

Booth, Gen. William, 145

Boyce, Dr. James, 29

Braden, Carl, 33

Brager, Carl, 31

Brooks, Fred, 32

Brown, H. Rap, 27, 35

Bruyn, Dr. Henry, 68

Bultmann, Rudolf, 114

California State Legislature, 18

California State College, Fullerton, 18

California, University of, 12, 68-69

Cambridge, Md., 27

capital punishment, 105, 110

Cardinal Mindszenty Foundation, 114-15

Carmichael, Stokely, 27-28, 30, 36, 96

Cassels, Louis, 114

Castro, Fidel, 76-77

Catholic Church, 83, 93, 114-119

Chambers, Whittaker, 63

Christian Church (Disciples), 98, 114

Cincinnati, Ohio, 27, 36

Clark, Gen. Mark, 47

Cleveland, Harlan, 64n.

Communist Party, U.S.A., 25-26, 34

Communist Party, USSR, 59

Commager, Henry Steele, 84

constitution, 105, 108-09

Coolidge, President Calvin, 128

Craig, May, 19-20

Crossroads, 115

Currie, Lauchlin, 63

Cuyahoga Co. Grand Jury, 25

de Tocqueville, Alexis, 20-21, 131

Detroit, Michigan, 28-31

disarmament, 155-56

Disciples of Christ, 98, 114

Dodd, Sen. Thomas, 72

Doll, Bishop Harry Lee, 98

Dooley, Dr. Thomas, 133-35

Douglas, Justice William, 161

Eisenhower, Pres. D. D., 48, 62, 135, 156

Elliot, Dr. Willis, 95

Episcopal Church, 95-96, 98-99, 102-04, 119

Evangelical United Brethren, 98

Fact the Nation, 60

Facelle, Thomas A. Jr., 71

Fair Play for Cuba Committee, 76-77

famine, 163

FBI, 30-31, 75, 101

Fletcher, Rev. Joseph, 96-97, 102

Ford, Cong. Gerald, 48

Fordham University, 83

Fort Lauderdale, Fla., 82-83

Franklin, Benjamin, 129-30
French Revolution, 129, 131
Fulbright, Sen. J. William, 61
Gary, Ind., 26
George, David Lloyd, 128
Glassboro, N.J., 59
Golding, Phil, 45
Goldwater, Barry, 142
Grant, Frederick, 117
Gross, Cong. H. R., 11, 53
Handbook for Christian Be-
  lievers, 113
Haiphong, 44, 45, 47, 134
Harper, Roger, 82
Harriman, Averrill, 60, 62
Harvard University, 68, 130
Henry, Patrick, 148
Hines, Bishop John, 95
Hiss, Alger, 62
Hitler, 62, 63
homosexuality, 99, 125, 161
Hoover, J. Edgar, 9, 14, 17,
  24-26, 29, 30, 37, 38, 69, 73,
  74, 75, 90, 96, 106
Humphrey, Vice President
  Hubert, 36, 60
Hunter, Lt. J. D., 45-46
inflation, 15-17
Indianapolis News, 52
Iowa State University, 68
Italian Communist Party, 76
Jamestown, Va., 107-08
Jefferson, Thomas, 20, 22
Job Corps, 81
Johnson, Pres. Lyndon, 10, 16,
  36, 43, 53, 56, 59, 81
Johnson, Manning, 38
Jones, Dr. E. Stanley, 91
Jones, LeRoi, 32
Karev, Rev. Alexander, 137
Kelleher, James, 81
Kennan, George, 58-59
Kennedy, Bishop Gerald, 114
Kennedy, Devereaux, 68
Kennedy, Sen. Robert, 12, 32,
  63, 136
Kerner, Gov. Otto, 30
Kim, Kyung Rai, 133

Kinnamon, Brice, 27
Khrushchev, Nikita, 62, 135
King, Martin Luther, 115, 136
Korea, 14, 15, 47, 133
Kosygin, Alexi, 50, 59, 135
Lady Chatterly's Lover, 74
Lanphier, Jeremiah, 144
Lenin, 14-16, 25, 33, 49
Lennon, John, 67
Lindsay, Mayor John, 34
Lipscomb, Cong. Glen, 52
Lomax, Louis, 28-29, 38-39
Los Angeles Times, 46
Louttit, Bishop Henry, 102
LSD, 68, 71
Luce, Philip Abbott, 24, 38
Luther, Martin, 112, 147
Lutheran Churches, 119
MacArthur, Gen. Douglas, 23,
  108, 128, 132
Maddocks, Rev. Lewis, 99
Magruder, F. A., 155
Marty, Dr. Martin E., 128
Marx, Karl, 33, 110, 112, 113
Marijuana, 71
McGill, Ralph, 136
McGuffey Readers, 84
McNamara, Robert S., 44
Meet The Press, 19, 30
Methodist Church, 81, 91, 116,
  117
Methodist Council on Evan-
  gelism, 116-117
Mikoyan, Anastas I., 61
Miranda decision, 39
Mobilization For Youth, 31
Moody, D. L., 145
Moody, Rev. Howard, 80
Narcotics, 71-72
NAACP, 30
National Council of Churches,
  91, 93, 94, 99, 100, 101, 122,
  125, 137, 160
National Science Foundation,
  52
Neighborhood Youth Corps, 34
New England Primer, 84
Newark, 11, 28

Newsweek, 30-31
Newton, John, 124
New York Board of Education, 70
New York Daily News, 31
New York Post, 31
New York Times, 13, 116
Nixon, Richard, 143
O'Boyle, Cardinal Patrick, 117
OEO, 11, 32-33, 81
Office of Economic Opportunity, 11, 32-33, 81
Oswald, Lee Harvey, 9
Otepka, Otto, 63
Panas, Walter, 71
Pastore, Sen. John, 64
People's Daily, 48
Philbrick, Herbert, 101
Pike, Bishop James, 124
Playboy, 80
Plymouth Colony, 107-108
Poland, 52
Pornography, 17-19, 74-77
Pope Paul, 117
Power failures, 35
Pravda, 51
Presbyterian Church, 91, 94-96, 98, 113, 115
Princeton Theological Seminary, 94
Protests, 69
Purdue University, 68
Puritan Ethic, 82, 108
Raichle, Frank, 79
Raines, Bishop Richard, 117
Ratliff, Thomas, 33
Reader's Digest, 15-17
Redbook, 77-78, 80, 82
Reston, James, 13
Rice, Msgr. Charles Owen, 93
Riesel, Victor, 32-33
Riots, 11-13, 21-42
Roman Catholic Church, 83, 93, 114-119
Roosevelt, Pres. Franklin, 57, 63
Rostow, Walt Whitman, 63
Roudebush, Cong. Richard, 52

Rusk, Dean, 50, 56-57, 63
Ryan, William, 48
Ryle, Bishop J.C., 125-126
Sabotage, 34-35
St. Louis Globe Democrat, 30, 69, 72, 84
St. Louis Post Dispatch, 27
Salinger, J.D., 17
Salvation Army, 145
Schlesinger, Arthur, Jr., 57-58, 113
Schott, Chief Jacob, 27, 36
Schrank, Robert, 34
Science & Mechanics, 50
Screvane, Paul, 24
Seeley, Dave, 68
Senate Internal Security Subcommittee, 76
Senate Preparedness Subcommittee, 43, 47
Shriver, Sargent, 11, 12, 32
Shaull, Prof. Richard, 94
slum clearance, 110
SNCC, 28, 69
Snyder, Rev. T. Richard, 94
Sorace, John, 32
Southern Baptist Convention, 99
Spock, Dr. Benjamin, 135-136
Stalin, Joseph, 57
Stang, Alan, 38
State Department, 60, 155
Stuart, Lyle, 76-77
Student Non-Violent Coordinating Committee, 28, 69
Supreme Court, 9, 10, 33, 74, 79
Symington, Sen. Stuart, 43, 47, 48
Taft, Sen. Robert A., 48
Thomas, Lowell, 71
Tillich, Paul, 114
Time Magazine, 163
Tito, 61-62
Tropic of Cancer, 74
Turkistan, 45
Ungersma, A.J., 113

Union Theological Seminary, 92-94

United Church of Christ, 95, 98, 99, 120

United Nations, 154, 155, 156, 157

United Planning Organization, 33

United Presbyterian Church, 91, 94-96, 98

United Press International, 13

University of California, 12, 68

U.S. Air Force, 51-52

U.S. Department of Commerce, 51

U.S. Department of State, 155

U.S. News & World Report, 34, 79, 100

U.S. Post Office, 74

U Thant, 155

Vance, Cyrus, 31

Vietnam, 9-11, 14, 15, 43-56, 69, 91, 133-135

VISTA, 33

Wade, Dr. Thomas, 71

Wang, Rev. Shih-ping, 132-133

Washington Evening Star, 38, 74

Washington University, 68, 74

WCC, 81, 93, 118

Wesley, John, 126-131, 140, 146-147

Westminster Confession of Faith, 120

Whan, Lee Chang, 133

White, Harry Dexter, 63

Whitefield, George, 126-131, 140

Wilkins, Roy, 29-30

Willis, Cong. E. E., 29

Winston, Henry, 34

Witt, Hal, 33

Witt, Nathan, 33

Wood, Rev. Frederick, 97-98

Word and Worship, 97, 114-115

World Council of Churches, 91, 93, 118, 137

World government, 153-157

Yale University, 73

Yalta, 57

Yalu River, 47

Younglove, Thomas, 35

Yugoslavia, 61-62

Another Liberty Bell Book

THE BLOOD OF JESUS

Written over 100 years ago in England, this is the story of a religious man who needed to be saved. Raised in the church, he came to realize one day that although he prayed, attended church and taught Sunday school that he didn't know God personally.

This personal story plus 12 short messages on why Jesus Christ shed His blood has sold millions of copies during the last 100 years.

Order copies for yourself, your church and friends.

PRICES

1 copy: $1 (including postage)

3 copies:	$2	10 copies:	$5
25 copies:	$10	100 copies:	$30
500 copies:	$125	1000 copies:	$200

ORDER FORM

LIBERTY BELL PRESS
Box 32, Florissant, Mo. 63032

Enclosed find $_____ for _____ copies of *The Blood of Jesus*. Ship postage-paid to:

Name_____

Street_____

City_____

State_____ Zip Code_____

Have you read...

NONE DARE
CALL IT TREASON

John Stormer's first book is a 7-million copy best seller. It carefully documents the communist infiltration of America's government, schools, churches, press, etc.

You can't understand what is happening in America and the world today until you've read it.

Order copies today for your self and friends.

PRICES

1 copy: $1 (including postage)

3 copies:	$2	10 copies:	$5
25 copies:	$10	100 copies:	$30
500 copies:	$125	1000 copies:	$200

ORDER FORM

LIBERTY BELL PRESS
Box 32, Florissant, Mo. 63032

Enclosed find $_____ for _____ copies of *None Dare Call It Treason*. Ship postage-paid to:

Name_____

Street_____

City_____

State_____ Zip Code_____

RECOMMENDED READING

COMMUNIST INFILTRATION
☐ None Dare Call It Treason, Stormer .... $ .75
☐ Color Communism and Common Sense, Johnson 1.00
☐ It's Very Simple, Stang 1.00
☐ Road To Revolution, Luce 1.00

See None Dare Call It Treason, pg. 254 for a list of 25 basic books on the influences of communism, socialism and liberalism in government, schools, churches, economics, etc.

CHRISTIAN READING

FOR THE SEEKER OR NEW CHRISTIAN
☐ What Christians Believe, Moody .... $ .50
☐ Talks To Men, Proofs of the Bible and
   Resurrection, Torrey 1.00
☐ The Blood of Jesus, Reid 1.00
☐ Cloud of Witnesses, McIntire 1.00

FOR SPIRITUAL GROWTH
☐ With Christ In The School of Prayer, Murray .... $ .60
☐ The Blessing of Pentecost, Murray 1.00
☐ Principles of Spiritual Growth, Stanford .... .60
☐ How To Win Souls, Lovett 1.00
☐ Vest Pocket Companion, A Handbook For
   Soul Winners, Torrey .... .50

Most of these paperback books can be obtained from Christian bookstores. This page may be used as an order form to obtain the books from Liberty Bell Press, Box 32, Florissant, Mo. 63032.

ORDER FORM

LIBERTY BELL PRESS
Box 32, Florissant, Mo, 63032

Enclosed find $_____ (add 10% for postage and handling) to cover the cost of the books checked on the above list. Send to:

Name_____

Street_____

City_____

State_____ Zip Code_____

------- ORDER FORM -------

Liberty Bell Press,
P. O. Box 32, Florissant, Mo., 63032

Send me _____ copies of **The Death Of A Nation.**

Payment of $ _____ is enclosed (send check or money order.)

Missouri residents add 3% sales tax.

Name _____

Street _____

City and State _____ Zip Code _____

HELP AWAKEN OTHERS!

Give

THE DEATH OF A NATION

To Friends, Relatives, Neighbors, Clergymen, School Teachers, Libraries.

Thousands of copies have already been distributed in every part of the United States. Doctors have given the book to members of their medical association. Businessmen have distributed them to members of their Chambers of Commerce. Individuals send them to employees in their companies, members of their churches, political and service organizations.

Do your part in this vital educational job. Order copies of *The Death Of A Nation* for your own use, at the low quantity prices below.

Order Form on Page 191

QUANTITY PRICES:

1 copy: $.75	10 copies: $5	100 copies: $30
3 copies: $2	25 copies: $10	500 copies: $125

1000 or more copies: $.20 ea.

Hard Cover Copies Available $2.95
12 or More Copies $2.95 each Less 40%

LIBERTY BELL PRESS
P. O. Box 32   Florissant, Mo.